MAX SHEPHE⌐ ⌐ROSS

Travels with Audrey

Contents

1	Introduction	1
2	Oxford	12
3	Meet Audrey	19
4	Preparation	38
5	Europe	50
6	Czech Republic	66
7	Romania	83
8	Bulgaria	88
9	Instanbul	93
10	Georgia	106
11	Azerbaijan	131
12	Police	142
13	Baku	150
14	Turkmenistan	164
15	Uzbekistan	190
16	Kazakhstan	232
17	Siberia	247
18	Mongolia	256
19	Epilogue	274

1

Introduction

It wasn't until the air outside was north of 40C that we began to understand the gravity of our situation. Not that our trip had been free from idiocy thus far, but it was on that damned sunbaked road in Azerbaijan that our number came up.

You see, when you fly into a distant land, you're hit by the cultural contrast like a smack in the face as soon as you leave the airport. That doesn't happen when you're driving — change happens gradually. Every day, the cultural norms, the languages and even the faces of the people you meet change ever so slightly, lulling you into a false sense of security that every day would be the same as the last.

We were driving east, heading for Baku and the Azerbaijani coast, where we had been assured a boat would be waiting for us to transport us (myself, Freddie, three Dutch hitchhikers on their way to Afghanistan "to have a look around," and a battered British ambulance called "Audrey") across the Caspian Sea and onwards to Turkmenistan.

Freddie, the only other person stupid enough to attempt this trip, leaned across to turn up the music, moaning along and banging his palms on the steering wheel, out of time, with the beat of the Rolling Stones or was it, Bowie? Not that it matters. The noise of the road drowned most of it, fortunately. Music has always been a source of energy for me. I need it to get going in the morning and to keep going throughout the day. And on a hot day like this with the windows down and desert air beating my face, only 70s rock will do.

Audrey, used to Manchester's cool climate and tarmacked roads, was persevering gallantly with few complaints as the unsealed road flung rocks up into her undercarriage. The central desert of Azerbaijan is a desolate place. Not like the deserts you see in the films, with graceful sand dunes and Arabs robed in all their splendour. Here the ground was tough and dead; the only marks on the landscape were the remnants of old rivers, dried out long ago, looking like they've been scraped down nearby hillsides by witches' fingernails.

I saw him first as we rounded the bend. One hand outstretched, marshalling us into a lay-by in front of his police station, the other resting on his gun. He wore an all-blue uniform, battered from years of service, buttons straining. His hair, what was left of it, greased into place. Aviator sunglasses plugged his eye sockets. Beside him was a younger and thinner version, but with twitching eyes and a tightly fitting matching blue baseball cap emblazoned with the word "POLIS".

I first got a look at his eyes as he peered over his aviators as he walked around the front of the van towards Freddie in the driver's seat. They were small, narrow, and focused. His gait was slow and methodical. His opposite number walked towards me looking over his shoulder for instruction.

"As-salāmu alaykum" we both said. The standard greeting we'd rehearsed countless times on our journey east from

2

Istanbul.

"Wa-alaikum As-salaam" they replied.

Niceties over, they made their move with assured confidence. He scanned the inside of the van for opportunities and pointed at our broken sat nav.

"TV, no," he said, wagging his index finger in Freddie's face.

It was not a TV, but a sat nav that has never worked. We wouldn't be here if it did. I'm sure he knew that, but that didn't seem to matter.

"TV, no!" He pointed again, voice raised.

Freddie, hitting the button beneath the screen, "Look, no work!" In that embracing English pigeon we all seem to adopt the moment we cross the channel.

"NO!" Now with his head and half his torso inside the window, leaning over Freddie.

"This is pointless," I said to Freddie, "He can't understand you. Let's just pay the bribe and get out of here. It's too hot to argue."

We were already two weeks behind schedule, and the ferry that represented our last chance of crossing into Central Asia was still half a day's drive away.

I reached into my wallet and pulled out the equivalent of a few US Dollars in Azerbaijani Manat.

I handed it over to his colleague on my side and flicked my hand at him to disappear like you do when you're hot, frustrated and dealing with an irritant.

He clasped his hand around mine as a smile spread across his face; I had fallen straight into his trap.

In one movement, he opened the door, pulled me out of the van and pushed me onto the floor. His heavy boots pressed against my back, and the roughness of the hot gravel road imprinted on my face.

"Well, that didn't go as planned, did it mate," said Freddie from a similar position from the other side of the van as they barked at us in Azerbaijani.

"I'm sure it's all part of the act; we'll be out here in no time," I shouted back, hoping he wouldn't pick up on the waver in my voice.

They pulled us up with our arms behind our backs, straining our chests, and frog-marched us towards the nearby station. A whitewashed building chipped in parts, it stood out against the beige of the desert like a last outpost from old Western movies. Every few steps, they shook us by violently pushing us forward and then pulling us back.

I was pushed through the station's front doors from behind, my face doing most of the opening against the hot steel of the door frame. It took me a while to adjust my sight, as I moved from the contrast of a bright forty-degree day to the cool shade of their station. A whitewashed room matching the exterior and a white tiled floor slowly emerged. It was bare apart from a desk at one end and the necessary picture of Ilham Aliyev, the 'democratically elected' ruler of Azerbaijan, adorning the wall behind it. Interior design, Azerbaijani style.

A snoozing junior officer jumped out of his seat in surprise as we were pushed down into two plastic chairs facing the desk. The chairs seemed intentionally smaller than usual, so once our friend, the commanding officer, took his seat, he glared down at us from above. If this was an attempt to unsettle us, it worked. His whipping boy, who had his palm pushing my face into the gravel of the road just minutes before, was standing to his right with his hands behind his back.

The boss forced his shirt buttons to work overtime as he

mopped away the sweat beading down his face and swatted away flies. His nose was stubby and small in contrast to the enormity of his round face. It seems deep insecurities are the driving force of police recruitment wherever you are in the world. There are few things more dangerous than a man who's had a rough lot in life when he's given an opportunity to recorrect the balance and assert his authority.

"These are purely intimidatory tactics, Freddie; we'll hang in and be out shortly" I whispered.

He didn't like that. Barking Azerbaijani in an unpleasant and irritated tone. When you're tasked with manning the empty hot roads of the Azerbaijani interior, an English numberplate is too much to pass on, I get that. We're just going to have to go along with the ride whilst he extracts his pound of flesh and American dollars. Hang in there, I told myself. I stared back at him, trying not to blink.

But my smug confidence only inflamed the situation. He wanted to see fear in our eyes. He wanted to feel, for that short moment, worth a dam.

You're going to have to work harder for that, mate.

With a resigned flick of his hand, his men got us up, and marshalled us through the back door and into the cell concealed behind. The door slammed behind us.

It was the first time I'd been in a cell, Freddie too. The all-too-familiar TV cop scene of a bare room with a solid door and a couple of plastic chairs was enough to scare the shit out of me and shake the false confidence from my bones.

Trying to lift our spirits, I told Freddie, "We should get a picture for our mums! They'd be so proud!"

But he barely smiled as he slid his back down the wall.

Time wore on and my mind darkened as a wave of hopelessness washed over me. What if this was more serious than we thought? When travelling from your armchair, you're always safe knowing that your British passport can get you out of any situation. But when you're here, and it happens to you in real life, doubts start creeping in. I wouldn't have thought "backpackers locked up in Azerbaijan" would garner much public sympathy. "Bloody idiots" would be the common and understandable response.

Without watches and with no clock in the room, neither Freddie nor I had any idea of how much time had passed when the door reopened, and the smaller of our captors marshalled us back to the two chairs in front of the desk. He was more hesitant than his boss; he wouldn't fix his gaze on us, his eyes shifting from side to side and then down to the floor. Nervousness? Or sorrow for what was about to happen?

Our passports were on the desk; they had been through the van.

I wonder if they've found the Dutchies? I thought. *It would look like we're running a fucking smuggling ring!*

We didn't know much about these Dutch guys — we had met Christaan, Joost and Bunk in the line for the Chinese Embassy in Georgia, where they had asked for a ride on route to Afghanistan. If the policeman had searched their bags and found vast quantities of stashed weed, it wouldn't have surprised me in the slightest.

We slumped back down into the small chairs that reminded me of the many I'd sat in school. Primary school. My back, soaked with sweat, stuck to the back of the chair. The temperature in the room had increased during our incarceration, and the fan above us just pushed hot air around the room with a dull whir.

The sergeant leaned over the desk, his hands supporting him, and looked back into my eyes and, after a while, smiled, finally seeing the fear he was after. He was winning and he knew it.

Our rap sheet had escalated far beyond the minor charge of watching TV whilst driving. But we had no idea what we were being accused of.

I scrambled my brain for the best way to salvage the situation. We needed to get hold of the British consulate in Baku to get a translator to at least understand the seriousness of all this. I had a list with all the embassies on our route, but it was back in the van on my phone.

If we were kept here for much longer, we would miss the ferry out of Baku, which would be our trip over. We'd given too much to let it slip away in the hands of a doughnut muncher. My phone was the only way out of this and I needed to get it.

I got up and walked as confidently as I could back towards Audrey. As I walked, the sergeant — in a state of shock — directed his junior to follow me.

I reached Audrey before he could catch up and got my phone out of the glove box. I raised my finger to him to gesticulate, "Just one second, please." The less confident of the duo consented. I scrolled through the list of British embassies I had jotted down. Azerbaijan was not among them.

Fuck.

There was shouting coming from within the station, which distracted the guard, and I used the moment to quickly text my dad.

Need number for the British embassy in Baku ASAP. Explain later
Probably not the message you want to receive from your son.

I left Audrey outside in the sun, our three Dutch stowaways still hiding, and re-entered the station. I could sense immediately that the power dynamic had shifted. Freddie had flipped. He was bent over the desk, screaming, his finger pointed in the face of the policeman, who had sat back down with a shocked look.

Whilst I was still trying to work out what the hell had happened, my phone pinged; it was a reply from dad. No questions, just the number of the embassy.

Jumping on Freddie's good work, I told our new friends, rather than asking them, that I was going to ring the British embassy.

I pressed dial, and after a few rings, I got an answer. A voice answered in the accent of a typical old boy of the Foreign Service. Queen's English and Union Jack boxers to match. An accent that would have irritated me back home, but today, in such foreign circumstances, I found it deeply reassuring. We've got someone on our side.

I explained the situation, to which the man on the end of the line sighed and asked to be passed across to whoever was in charge. I did so. The sergeant, who was now sitting back in his chair, raised his eyebrows, exhaled and then conceded and grabbed the phone.

I felt that we were slowly clawing at the bastard's balance of power.

After a short conversation, the phone was passed back. I put it to my ear.

"Listen, boys, it seems you've got yourself in a bit of a tricky spot," the man at the embassy explained. "They're accusing you of trying to bribe a public official, and from what I can see, they've got fairly strong evidence. This is a very serious charge in Azerbaijan."

"We'll open up the usual channels here in Baku, but if you've done what they say you've done, there's not much we can do for you."

His previously reassuring voice now turned into something more sinister. I felt like we were in the middle of a John le Carré novel, being left out in the cold by our own team. I half expected him to say, "Sorry old chap, toodle-pip.."

I put down the phone and looked back to the sergeant, who, realising we had finally got it, smiled back at me contentedly with his arms crossed over his belly.

After relaying the damning inditement to Freddie, I look down to the floor. Now it was me mopping my brow and swatting away the incessant flies.

We were led back to the cell, where we both sat in silence for some time.

My mind raced: how could we have been so stupid? We were just a bunch of naive Westerners, thinking we could rely on the stereotype and throw money at any problem. I felt stupid and embarrassed. I'd always thought I was better than that. More "worldly", more understanding of other cultures. But it turns out I'm just another affluent cliché. No better than those tourists I'd scoffed at on the news for getting banged up for getting too drunk in Thailand or Vietnam.

After an age, Freddie spoke.

"All of this for two fucking dollars. I mean, they can't prosecute us for just two dollars, can they?"

I shrugged. Then something twigged. "What if we just didn't bribe enough? What if this has just been a huge charade to get us just to give them more cash?"

Freddie looked at me incredulously.

"You're suggesting that, from inside a cell where we're being held for trying to bribe police officers, that we...try to bribe them again? Pretty risky strategy, mate!"

"Well, what else have we got?" I asked. He shrugged.

And so, a plan was hatched. We would knock on the door and hand them back our passports with $200 tucked inside. The $200 amount was intensely discussed but had little logic. If they kicked up a fuss, we would claim that we were just keeping it in there for safekeeping. It was a weak story at best, but it was all we had. It sounds so stupid now, with so much potential to blow up in our faces, but the level of hopelessness we were feeling drove us to believe it was possible.

In for a penny, in for a pound. Idiots.

Freddie knocked on the door; the noise seemed to boom through the quiet station. The sergeant across from the entrance to our cell looked up in surprise, annoyed to have his attention drawn away from his book. He walked over slowly, and after pausing to reconsider, Freddie put his passport through the hatch in the door, and time slowed to a crawl. As the sergeant's hand moved up to take the passport, my heart was in my mouth, I reached out to grab it back, but it was too late. He slowly peeled through page after page, stamped haphazardly with visas from each country we'd passed through on our way here. He stopped as he reached the money. The rest of the trip, hell, the rest of our twenties, depended on this moment.

He took the money into his hand and then looked up at us. Slowly, a smile cracked over his face. He opened the cell.

"Gentlemen..." he said, in his newly found English, "Wel-come to Azerbaijan,", and marshalled us towards the door. His smile smug. He laughed as we walked out of the station. He had played his hand well, and he'd won.

But we didn't care; our ordeal was over. We walked back to Audrey, giving each other a hug that was a mixture of consolation and relief. We had been kippered, well and truly. But just two minutes ago, we were sizing up decades in the slammer. And now to be back with Audrey; to put her into first gear; to feel the warm desert air through our hair once more as we drove away; that felt like a win. Our big gamble had paid off.

Now, why were we driving through the Azerbaijani desert in a battered up British ambulance with three Dutch guys in the back? To answer that we need to go back a month, to Oxford, England and our last day of university.

2

Oxford

Fred and I were slumped in our seats in the Rusty Bicycle in Oxford, nursing half- empty pints.

What had started as a celebratory drink had deteriorated sharply with the realisation that graduation signalled the end of Uni and the start of "corporate annual leave policies" and "contracted working hours."

"This is depressing," Freddie muttered as he slid further into his chair. "This is the last summer we can do anything without asking permission from some egotistical corporate zombie." (Our prejudice against everyday working life would later prove surprisingly accurate).

We had two weeks until graduation and then two months until our jobs — we had both accepted positions at big corporate organisations in London — starting in September.

"We're going to have to go out in style...." I said. "What are you thinking? Travelling?"

"Yeah, but I want to do something more than the standard 'getting-pissed-in-a-hostel- whilst-trying-to-find-yourself' trip."

The standard answer to such a predicament was to pack up a backpack and jet off to Thailand, South America, or Australia. Or Cambodia, if you were ahead of the curve. And then come back and wear your Bin-tang singlet, keep your dreadlocks and call everyone "man" for the next six months. But that felt "done" and uninspiring. The most significant danger you faced on such trips was getting locked out of your hostel room. No, to get us out of this particular fud, we needed something more; we needed a real adventure.

"What then? Road trip?" Freddie said. "Would have to be a big one."

"What's the furthest you can drive from Oxford?" "Dunno... Spain, maybe?" said Freddie.

"Oh, come on, we must be able to get further than Europe!" I replied.

Fred leaned forward in his chair, showing more energy than in the previous three hours. "Okay, let's plan. I'll get two more pints. You get the map out on your phone," he said.

Fred went up to the bar with renewed vigour.

As two pints landed back on our table, sloshing beer as they arrived, I got out my phone, opened Maps and zoomed out so we could see all of Europe.

"Okay then..." I said. "we can actually cross the channel at Dover and then head up through Eastern Europe and into Russia, and from there, you could go anywhere, really."

"Huh, interesting", Freddie replied.

"Or you can go south to Turkey through the length of Europe. Now that is interesting; I've always wanted to go to Istanbul."

"What's the next country along from Turkey?" Freddie said. "Iran!" I replied.

13

"I've always wanted to go to Iran! "Okay, this is getting interesting now."

We gulped down our pints in a fraction of the time it took us to drink the previous. Our eyes open wide, bodies forward in our chairs, crouching over the table where my phone lay.

"Okay, where next?"

I traced my finger along the screen.

"Well, the next country is either Afghanistan or Turkmenistan," I said.

"Well, we're currently at war with Afghanistan, and I've never heard of Turkmenistan!" said Freddie.

With that, I looked up Turkmenistan on my phone.

The least country visited in the world" was the first result. "Interesting!" we both shouted.

"One of the last true dictatorships in the world" was the second result. "Even more interesting!" we both chimed again.

"If we want an adventure, that's where we can find it," said Freddie. "Okay, what's next?" Freddie continued

I traced my finger along further. "From there, we can head north to Uzbekistan, and from there, Kazakhstan.."

"We can go see Borat!" Freddie interrupted with a squeal.

"Ha-ha, yes!" and with that, we cheers'd our pint glasses. "To Turkmenistan and to Borat!" we shouted in unison, splashing beer over my phone and shattering the typically calm surroundings of the Rusty Bicycle as nearby pensioners peered over their glasses at us.

"We're going to Turkistan!" I shouted back, raising my glass in one hand, and spilling beer down my arm.

"No, it's Turkmenistan, you idiot," Freddie corrected.

"Turkmenistan! "

To which the old man shook his head and returned to his

reading.

Not letting that stop our fun, we looked back to the beer-soaked phone. "Okay, okay, where next?"

"Well, from there, we can cross into Siberia." "Wow, Siberia, that sounds remote".

"Okay, and then where?" Freddie said, continuing our fun. "Well, then we can go to Mongolia."

"Oh, wow, that's meant to be beautiful."

"And then we can just cross into China, and then, wow, you're at the Pacific Ocean." "The Atlantic to the Pacific — now *that* is a road trip." Freddie proclaimed.

And with that, we cheers'd our glasses one more time to make it official and stumbled home to bed.

"We must tell the others in the morning," I whispered as we got home trying not to wake our housemates. "Good idea!" Freddie replied.

* * *

The following day, I woke with a pounding headache and a throat like a desert. I reached for a glass of water and gulped it down. I laid back in my bed and stared at the ceiling, groaning. But then I remembered.

"Freddie!" I shouted and kicked off the duvet and ran into his room.

"Fuck off!" Freddie shouted, clearly feeling the same effects as me, as I burst into his room.

"Mate, don't you remember!" And with that, he sat bolt upright. "Oh yes! We have to tell the others! They'll love it."."

We went downstairs to find George and Jon playing FIFA in our bare student house. Two sofas, a TV and a PlayStation, were the sum total of our decorations. What else do you need? We had all just graduated from Oxford Brookes. A university whose sole value lies in the fact that every now and again, someone gets confused and thinks you went to the "other" Oxford. Plunging you into a moral conundrum of whether to correct them. I rarely do, particularly in job interviews.

"Boys, we've had a hell of an idea."

"Yes? " Jon replied without taking his eye off the game.

"Well, you know it's our last year of freedom," kicking off the pitch. "Freedom from what?" Jon replied.

"Our jobs! We can't ever travel again!"

"Calm down, mate, we can still go on holiday," Jon didn't share my corporate annual leave allowance concerns.

"Yeah, but not really, not properly," I said. "Okay, anyway, we want to go out in style."

"We're going to drive from Oxford to Beijing. The Atlantic to the Pacific," Freddie interrupted, sensing I was losing the room.

Silence.

"You're both fucking idiots," George replied as he scored the winning goal. To be fair, George hadn't gone further east than Cambridge. So perhaps he wasn't our target market.

I turned to Jon, "What do you think?" "Are you being serious?"

"Yes, of course! Why wouldn't we be?'

"I don't let Freddie drive me to Tesco, let alone Beijing! Anyway, what are you going to drive? Freddie's Corsa?" Jon replied.

A fair question; we hadn't thought about that in all our excitement.

Resigned, I went and switched the kettle on and turned to Freddie. "Okay, maybe we need to think about this more when I've got less of a headache."

"I think that's a very good idea," Jon shouted from the next room. He was always the sensible one of the bunch. Annoyingly.

With coffee in place of beer, we sat down again that afternoon to walk through the previous night's plans without the same vigour.

"Okay, so was this just a drunken idea or are we actually going to try and do this?" I started.

"Well, I'm still keen," replied Freddie, "I've got nothing else to do with my summer."

"Okay, me too. A few things we need to think through. One, how long will it take? We've got jobs starting in September, and being late on our first day wouldn't be good."

"Especially if we're a month late," Freddie interjected. "Indeed."

"What's next?"

"What are we going to drive?"

"Well, that's easy; a VW Camper. I've always wanted one, and we can save money on hostels," said Freddie.

"Okay, finally, visas. I have no idea where to start with that one." "Me neither."

"Right, we'll divide and conquer. You tackle the car, and I'll tackle the visas and the distance."

We returned thirty minutes later in a deadlock. Firstly, VW Camper's cost £10,000.

£10,000 of which we did not have after three years of amass-ing student debts. Secondly, it was 12,000 miles to Beijing, at 125 miles a day, that would be just over three months of driving. We would have to leave in two weeks if we were to stand any chance of getting back for our jobs. Finally, visas were required for every country east of Turkey, and each of them required an in-person embassy visit. Not to mention the fact that the British government advised against travel to every one of them.

3

Meet Audrey

Now, I've read similar travel stories before; they all start by boring you senseless with their endless months of preparation and planning. So much so that it seemed to suck any joy out of the trip.

So fortunately for you, dear reader, I'm not going to do that. It is partly because it is as boring to write it as it is to read it. And I have a notoriously low boredom threshold. But mostly because we did, looking back now, a worryingly little amount of planning.

There are, however, a few essential aspects that need to be covered that will provide context for our future trials and tribulations on the road—mostly revolving around our choice of car and our lack of visas.

Let's firstly cover the car.

As previously mentioned, we didn't realise on that first booze-soaked planning session in the Rusty Bicycle that VW campers cost £10,000. After three years of amassing impressive student debts, that was ten grand that we did not have. Not even close.

A significant early roadblock.

We entertained the prospect of doing it in a normal car. In reality, it was a non-starter. I shared a car with my mum and my brother (I didn't ask), and Freddie's car was a 750cc Corsa that wouldn't have made it past Dover. On top of that, it would also mean spending a lot more on hotels en route, *which* meant more money. Not to mention the hellish picture of spending three months in a hatchback with Freddie.

A few days later, Freddie had a brain wave. I got a call from him in the early hours, walking back from a night out in a state of complete excitement.

"Mate, an ambulance has just driven past me."

It's best to humour Freddie when he's in this mood, so I let him continue rather than putting the phone straight down and going back to sleep.

"Right...and?" Already regretting my decision.

"They're basically the same shape as a VW camper! We could buy a retired ambulance and strip it out. Convert it into a camper."

"Can you even buy an ambulance?! Do they retire ambulances?" "I don't know; ring up the hospital in the morning."

Click.

I reminded myself never to answer calls from Freddie when he'd been drinking.

* * *

"Good morning, Oxford John Radcliffe."

"Erm, hi. weird question, but what happens to your ambulances after you've finished with them?" As soon as the words left my mouth, I wondered how the hell Freddie had convinced me to do this.

"Excuse me?" replied the baffled nurse.

Getting pretty embarrassed now and wishing I could just hang up and forget the whole idea, I nonetheless continued. "When your ambulances get too old, what happens to them?"

"Do you realise this phone line is for patients to speak with their doctors, sir?" The words leaving her mouth forcibly now.

"Oh, sorry, no, I didn't. It's the only number I could find. Is there anyone there who can help, please?" Really, really, wishing I had just ignored Freddie now. Or better, made him do it. Why do I always get carried up in his ideas?

"Hold on."

I looked at Freddie. We might be onto something here.

The woman hadn't bothered to put me on hold; I imagined her clasping her hand over the mouthpiece. I heard her talking to a colleague in the background.

"Eric! There's someone asking about our old ambulances on the phone. Yes, I told them this is the doctor's line." I don't think she cared if I heard her conversation or not.

I couldn't hear Eric's part of the conversation, but after a while, she came back on the line.

"Apparently, we sell them to specialised dealers." "Great — do you know what their contact details are?"

"No, I don't! Now I really need to get back to helping patients."

"Do you mind asking your colleague again? I would really appreciate it," fearing I had gone one step too far now.

She sighed. "Eric! What's the dealer called?" I heard a

muffled reply. "They're called UK Ambulance Sales."

"Thank-" Click.

And with that, the call was over.

I turned to Freddie, who looked smug that both his plan worked, and he didn't have to follow them through. "With a name like that, we could probably just have Googled it," I said.

"I think that was her point," Freddie replied.

UK Ambulance Sales was a scrapyard based in Dartford, where NHS ambulances go to die. Their retirement home and final resting place.

After giving them a call, we drove down there the next day. On our journey down, we were in a state of complete excitement. Our dream for that summer was alive again after lying dead in a ditch as the costs mounted. It turns out you can get a "brand new" retired ambulance for £2,000. A snip compared to the £10k for the VW. This was still way out of budget, but it was, at least, a little closer.

We arrived at the dealership and met the owner, David. You've probably never imagined the type of person that sells retired ambulances. But if you did, I'm quite sure you would imagine David. A tall, well-built man in his 50s with hands rough from tinkering with ambulances all day. He had the edge of a second-hand car salesman but the geekiness of a stamp collector. And, boy, did he know his ambulances. Without invitation, he proceeded to tell us about every make and model of serving British ambulance, whether he had it in stock or not.

We walked around this graveyard of sorts as he gave his lecture. Ambulance after ambulance was parked in line after line; it was quite a sight. Each relic was in a different state of disrepair. Ranging from gleaming, recently washed vehicles that looked like they saved their last patient just last night to some that were barely recognisable as ambulances. Their bodies had been ripped off, and their insides mined for scraps.

"Some come here unrepairable, you see, so I just use them for spare parts to patch up the saveable ones," he continued. "The paramedics give them a really rough time," he said as if he was talking about an abused dog. "They drive them at crazy speeds and slam them into corners. They're medics, not mechanics, you see," he gazed wistfully over his family of strays.

We turned a corner, and there she stood. I knew immediately she was the one. I don't know what it was exactly, but I knew.

"What about that one?" I asked.

"Ah, one of my very best", he looked on proudly. "A Renault Master from Manchester. She served the Manchester Royal Infirmary for ten years." I almost expected him to shed a tear in pride.

"She was fairly beaten up when she arrived, but I patched her back together, didn't I, darling?" He patted the ambulance affectionately on her bonnet and gazed into the windshield at her imaginary eyes.

Fred and I walked around her. She was white, as you might imagine, with yellow stripes across the top of her sides and roof, with bright blue lights. Getting closer, she was badly rusted on her underside and sported the bruises from ten years of skating around Manchester's roads in the early hours of the morning.

We opened up the back door. To my amazement, everything was still there apart from the stretcher. The paramedic's chair sat side-on and medicine cupboards covered in soft green padded material, I assume to stop heads bashing against them at high speed, lined every part of the internal walls.

We climbed back out and kicked her tyres (literally) to try and make it look like we hadn't already made up our minds. The just visible words "Emergency Vehicle" and "Ambulance" were emblazoned on her side and printed backwards on her bonnet, showing her undoubted pedigree but also that she was ready for a new life and role within it. Like a champion racehorse ready to be the first steed of a young girl. It was clear she was calm-headed and reliable in a crisis, but there was a glint in her eye that hinted she was capable of more. She possessed something in spades that was more important than any other feature or dull specification: character.

I opened the door and jumped into the driver's seat. When I first turned the key in her ignition, she thought about it first like a dog sniffing your hand to judge whether to trust you. She took her time, and when she was good and ready and sure of me, she consented and turned her large Renault engine over for the first time. And once she started, she didn't so much as purr but fight for attention. Her revs loud and hostile, like a greyhound straining on the leash before a race.

It was a wise strategy from her (she always was a "her," I can't tell you why I'll leave that to mystery and intrigue). Any customer preparing for a lesser trip, where character wasn't of utmost importance, would have cast her aside as unreliable. She was looking for us as much as we were looking for her.

If you were to describe her, the words "beautiful," "stunning", and "eye-catching" would not spring to mind. But rather, "wholesome," "strong", and "dependable". For want of a better word, she was big-boned, broad, almost two and a half meters wide, but supremely strong, capable of carrying

1,200 kg. The rust under her belly and dents
to her chassis showed her years but also her wisdom and experience. She gave me supreme confidence that she would rise to any challenge we faced.

Sitting in the driver's seat, gazing out through the windshield, a buzz of excitement rushed over me. I had visions of foreign lands stretching out in front of us. I caught Freddie's eye from the passenger seat; I could tell he was feeling the same. For the first time, it felt like our trip was going to happen.

And then I saw it. A blue button that said "Siren" on it. I gasped. "Do they still work?!"

Before David had a chance to reply, I pushed it.

I jumped out of my seat as the sirens started their wail. They stuttered at first but then grew in confidence as they gained full voice. The blue lights started flashing. So bright I could see the beams of light hit neighbouring vehicles.

I instinctively patted her dashboard. She was just perfect.

I tried to regain my composure to not give him the edge in negotiations.

"How much?" I asked, trying to be as casual as possible and not looking him in the eye.

"£2,000," he replied.

I didn't care; she would be ours at any price.

Freddie, less liable to be swept up in emotion and feeling, took a more pragmatic approach.

"Wow, that's a lot," he jumped in, taking over negotiations.

"How would you know what an ambulance costs?" David replied. Fair point.

"Are you sure there was no wiggle room?" Freddie continued. "Quite sure."

"How about £1,750?" "£2,000."

"£1,800?"

"£2,000."

Okay, this isn't working; let's try a new tact. "We'll have to think about it at that price," I said. "Okay, you've got my number."

Damn, he called our bluff.

Fred and I decamped to a nearby pub to debrief. Two pints and two burgers were ordered.

I took a sip of my beer. "What do you think, mate?" I asked. "I don't know; two grand is a lot."

"I know, but she's just perfect. Did you see all her cupboards? And the siren actually works! Imagine how much time we can save in traffic!"

"Ha-ha, calm down, mate. I'm just trying to think about the cost. We don't have two grand!"

"I know," I sighed. "There must be a way." I racked my brains. "What if we sell advertising on the side? We're sure to get some press?"

"I'm not so sure," Freddie cautioned. At that moment, my phone rang.

"Hello?" It was David the ambulance salesman.

"Hi Max, we've just had an offer on the Renault Master you were looking at. I said to myself I'd be fair and offer you the first crack as you saw her first. They've offered

£2,000, so she's yours for £2,100. But no worries if you're not interested." "No, I am interested, absolutely. Don't give it to them! We'll take her!" Fred put his head in his hands.

"Great, I'll text you the details. Payment within twenty-four hours." I put the phone down and sheepishly looked at Freddie.

"You do realise that's the oldest trick in the book, don't

you mate?" Freddie said. "Yes, I do realise that now," I said, looking down at my pint.

"Okay, so how do we get £2,000?" Freddie said with his eyebrows raised while taking a sip of his beer.

"£2,100," I replied. "What?"

"We need £2,100. I agreed to pay £2,100. And I agreed to pay it in twenty-four hours."

Fred put his pint down and stared at me.

* * *

The next day Freddie and I set up a call centre in our university kitchen. Immune to the obvious complaints from our house-mates and fuelled by coffee, we sat in front of our laptops and called around every business in Oxford, offering them a "once in a lifetime" sponsorship opportunity. For a mere £1,000, they could receive coverage from Oxford to Beijing.

"How many can we fit?" asked Freddie.

"I don't think that's going to be a problem," I replied after a flurry of quite rude rejections.

"The only way that Ambulance is getting to Beijing is in a fucking box," was a typical response, promptly followed by the person on the other end of the line hanging up.

Even our local off-licence and kebab house, that we had supported loyally throughout our whole tenure, said no.

Two hours before our payment deadline and after yet another rejection, Freddie turned to me, "I think we need to move to plan B, mate; tapping up our family."

"Have you got any family members with businesses?" I replied.

"No, but you have."

"Yes, thanks for that." Once again, it fell to me to make the call.

I had two chances, my uncle, who owned a financial reporting firm called TS Lombard and my dad, who ran a fire alarm business. As far as I was aware, none of them had or had any interest in having, clients along our route. And in my Dad's case, outside of Cheltenham, the small town where I was brought up.

I started with the easier of the two targets, my uncle. I picked up the phone and already felt ashamed for the lies I was about to tell.

"Hi, Uncle Nick" "Max! How are you?"

"I'm very well, I hope you are too. Now listen, Nick, I've got a very attractive proposition for you. I wanted to tell you about before offering it to the wider business community. We're driving from Oxford to Beijing in an ambulance."

"You're doing what?!" he replied with a snort. "Why on earth are you doing that?!"

"Well, I'll get to that in a minute, but first we're speaking to a number of newspapers about covering the trip, *The Times* being one of them."

"Oh, really?"

"Yes, and...um...we are selling advertising space on the side of the van that will be displayed prominently in any such coverage. Not to mention the coverage you will get from all passers-by between here and Beijing."

"Most of whom can't speak English," he interjected.

"Well, I wouldn't be so sure. The world's a small place these days. But of course, there's obviously been a lot of interest, so if you're not interested…"

"I thought you hadn't offered it to anyone else yet?" "Well, just to a few peo—"

"How much?"

"We were thinking around £1,000," trying to sound confident in our valuation.

"If you can get into *The Times*, I'll give you £500 for the space." "Done!" I shouted, thanked him a little too profusely and hung up.

Freddie looked at me with astonishment. "How the hell did you pull that off?"

"I'm surprised you have to ask, Freddie," I said, looking at him as if he should be well aware of my powers of persuasion.

"But seriously, mate."

"I promised we would get into *The Times,* with his logo."

For the second time in twenty-four hours, Freddie put his drink down and stared at me incredulously.

I ignored his bemusement and picked my phone back up full of confidence. "Okay, now for the tricky one; Dad."

I selected his name and dialled.

"Hi Dad," I said, trying to sound cheerful. "You know this trip Freddie, and I are planning?"

"Yes, I've been speaking with your mother about that," he replied.

I cleared my throat; this might be a tricky call. "Well, we are selling advertising space on the side of the van, and we've had a lot of interest…"

"That's bollocks, and you know it," my Dad interjected. "Well, I'm not so sure…"

"I am. Anyway, why were you talking to me about it?"

"Well, in your position as a business owner, I thought you might like, or be interested in, you know?"

"I know what?"

"Buying a space. It would be perfect for Firecall." "Not on your life."

"Oh."

"But this trip of yours, how long will it take?" "Just over three months"

"You'll be gone all summer? You won't be moping around the house?" "Well, if we can pay for the ambulance, yes."

"Right, I'll give you £500 just for that. Bargain."

"Great! Thank you! Do you want to put your logo on the side?" "Not really."

"Okay, well, thanks anyway."

I looked at Fred, "Another £500."

Fred raised his eyebrows as if to say "And...?" "Nope, no strings attached this time, weirdly..."

"Huh. Well, that's £1,000 in total. If we put in £550 each, she's ours." "The last cheque of our student loan should just about cover that." "Let's ring up the dealer and lock her down!"

A few days later, I hopped into the front seat of our prized new ambulance, put my hands on her steering wheel and got the buzz of excitement all over again. She was even better than I remembered. Dressed in perfect white, a big brute of a vehicle that I felt sure would protect against any and all foes on the road.

"You know, for the first time, I'm starting to think we might actually do this, you know," Freddie said after taking his position in the passenger seat.

"Well, if we don't, I have no idea what we'll do with a £2,000 ambulance," I replied. "£2,100." Freddie corrected, with a lingering edge of frustration.

I rubbed my hand up and down the dashboard. "I think we should call her Audrey," I said, "Audrey the Ambulance."

It would be fair to say that we took a relaxed approach to our route planning. Writing this now, it feels deeply foreign and ancient that we couldn't just fire up Google Maps, type "Beijing' and be on our way. But Google Maps wasn't what it is now. I was a proud owner of a Blackberry at the time; remember those? And you couldn't just head down to your local petrol station and buy a road map of Turkmenistan or Siberia. But fortunately, there was a place where you could.

* * *

The Stanfords map shop in Covent Garden is a magical place. Amazingly they only sell maps, or they did when we went. Going down the steps into their basement was like descending into the world of a Victorian explorer, like Scott of Antarctica's basement. There were maps of every corner of the world plastered to the walls; many weren't even made this century. What use people find in old maps of long-since disappeared roads and buildings was a question worth considering. But there they were.

We collared a sales assistant who looked incredibly bored after describing to a 45- year-old accountant the difference between various maps of the Home Counties.

He soon perked up, however, when we gave him our long

list of maps that we required. "I have never been asked for a map of Turkmenistan before!" He proclaimed. "But don't worry, we'll have it somewhere." And with that, off he beetled excitedly.

He returned, straining under the weight of 40 or so maps, grinning from ear to ear. "I think we just made his day," I said to Freddie as we walked out of the store after bearing the considerable cost of our purchase.

We rushed home to start planning our route. Full of excitement, we opened the maps and spread them over the kitchen table. There's something about those Stanford maps. It's not like picking up your dad's never-used road map that he left in your car for emergencies; they have a magic quality about them. Looking over a map of an unknown land fills me with a feeling of excitement and possibility. The colours highlight a change in landscape, the foreign place names, and the contours showing deep ravines. The more foreign and dangerous, the more colourful they become. I love every bit of them.

Europe looked easy, almost boring. Beautifully tarmacked roads paved our route from England to Turkey. We would have our pick of campsites and hostels to sleep in, restaurants to eat in, and bars to quench our thirst.

We would start by taking the ferry from Dover in the south of England across to Calais in the north of France. We would then take a left through Belgium, Germany, and then turn immediately south through the ancient capitals of the Czech Republic, Austria, and Hungary, then take in the old Soviet belt that's now known as Slovakia. After that, we'd head south, tracing the coast of the Black Sea through Romania, and Bulgaria and then leaving Europe and entering Asia by crossing the Bosporus straight into Istanbul and continuing east by following the southern coast of the Black Sea.

From there, it got a little trickier. At the edge of Turkey sat the ancient and mysterious, and politically interesting Iran. Iran had the honour of being our first country on the UK Do Not Travel list, which estimated the risk of terrorism as "very likely." However, it wasn't a hare-brained death wish destined for the ten o'clock news that piqued our interest. I'd grown up in a house stuffed full of National Geographic magazines that told romantic stories of the oldest civilisation on earth living between turquoise-domed mosques and glittering palaces. My ten-year-old self couldn't imagine anything more foreign and exciting.

From there, we would pass into the secretive dictatorship of Turkmenistan, tracing the Afghani border through Uzbekistan. At which point, it looks like you get a clear shot of Beijing by crossing into China and driving straight through the belly of the colossal country. However, you were blocked by the small matter of the Himalayas. We were reliably informed by our maps that there was no way through, and in actual fact, the border into China was completely closed off. So instead, you have to turn north and drive up through Kazakhstan and keep going way up into the wasteland of Siberia and then turn back down south onto the Mongolian Steppe which then, finally, gives you a clear shot of Beijing, through the Gobi Desert.

It was the second half of the trip that was causing us some alarm. We were happy to take the odd risk; anyone who attempts a trip like this probably is, but skirting a full-scale war zone was taking things a bit far.

It wasn't so much the risk of being shot at that worried us, as we were pretty confident that we would be able to avoid the actual areas of fighting. It was more the likely the frosty reception we would get from the locals if our government were in the process of bombing their towns, villages and schools.

In any case, our hands were tied. The route would pick us. And we sought solace in the fact that if the omens were dark, they were at least vigorous and exciting.

Looking back now, I wonder if we sought out this danger, subconsciously or not. There were a million different road trips we could have chosen, yet we ended up choosing some of the most dangerous countries on the planet. What's in that? Perhaps there was a small nagging desire at the back of our mind that if all didn't go to plan, at least we would return with an interesting story or two. Or perhaps we just wanted to see the world portrayed to us through the evening news up close. The key would be to find a balance between excitement and disaster.

In any case, we estimated, depending on the route chosen, the journey would take us between fifty-five and sixty-five days, give or take twenty or so days.

Our favourite thing to do was to lay out our beautiful maps end to end across Freddie's kitchen floor and into his sitting room and out into the garden so that our whole route was shown in miniature scale. Those maps have an amazing beauty to them. It felt like we were one of the famous explorers of England's past when this sort of endeavour was undertaken by gentlemen and met with a front-page article in *The Times* and a send-off by a thousand adoring fans.

When we stood above it and traced our route by walking through the entirety of Freddie's kitchen, living room and garden, the enormity of the challenge would hit us.

The ever-changing colours of the map, from the bright green of England to the brown and dark yellow of the deserts of central Asia and back again, highlighted the physical, not to mention political, variety we were heading for.

With our route mapped out, the next phase of our preparations was getting the relevant visas. The excitement was fast rising, in our heads, we were already whizzing through European meadows, windows down, sunglasses on, and *Summertime* blaring from the radio. But getting the required visas turned out to be a complete shit show.

In order to get back in time for our graduate jobs, we only had two days to visit all the seven necessary embassies before we had to leave. Helpfully, the embassies were scattered across London and we both needed to be there in person. We scheduled back-to-back meetings, with an ambitious fifteen minutes to get between each one. Everything had to go like clockwork. It didn't.

After a long night of route planning while staying at a friend's house in London, I woke up with a groan in my stomach that you only get from oversleeping. That split second when you wake up and realise, deep in your stomach, that you're already late, is there a worse feeling in the world? I scrambled out of bed and threw on clothes in the order I found them whilst shouting at Freddie in the next room. We raced down to the tube, but we knew it was already too late. We had missed our meeting at the Chinese and Mongolian embassies. Two of the big ones. Mongolia was our only way into China unless we wanted to cross the Himalayas (we didn't, and Audrey certainly didn't). And you definitely can't get to Beijing without going through China.

Unfortunately for us, we couldn't rebook an appointment at either embassy for another month. "We'll get them on the way," we thought, "They must have embassies in the countries we're travelling to..." As we ran out of Knightsbridge tube station on to our next appointment; Turkmenistan.

The Turkmenistan embassy was housed in one of the four-storey white Georgian townhouses that are typical of West London. Once the homes of the great and good of high society, now stuffed full of cheap hotels, internet cafes with questionable sources of revenue and the embassies of banana republics.

The great thing about the Turkmenistan embassy was that not a lot of people want to go to Turkmenistan, so the queue was short. So much so, we walked in and sat down straight away with the relevant man. Despite our late start, I thought we'd make good time here and be able to catch up on the day. How naive.

The embassy official was squeezed into a suit that reflected the harsh neon lighting back at us as we sat down in his basement office. He stared back through us with an unfocused gaze; the look of a man forced to live side by side with us capitalist pigs by his government for too long.

We handed our passports across to him and smiled expectantly.

He exhaled, "we don't issue tourist visas without a government minder being present at all times," were the first words out of his mouth in a monosyllabic tired tone.

Ouch, probably should have checked that before we came.

"Can we get a government minder, then?" we replied, expectantly, hoping that he'd take pity on two naive students who wanted to visit his homeland and learn the virtues of the dictatorship.

His face efficiently conveyed that not only was that not

possible, but also that his patience was rapidly wearing thin. His eyes followed us as we sheepishly got up and shuffled out of the room.

It was nearly lunchtime, and we didn't yet have a visa to show for our efforts. We would have to find another way through. But there was no time to think about that for the moment, we had to get across town to our final two appointments at the Uzbek and Kazakh embassies. Our plan was blowing up in our faces, but we forged on.

After a morning of misfires, the Uzbeks and the Kazakhs could not have been more pleasant and cheerful. Two stamps of our passports and two tourists' visas handed over with a smile and a limited amount of fuss. This was more like it.

But it had been an emotionally exhausting day as we dissected our efforts from a nearby pub. "Two out of five isn't great" was Freddie's review. It was hard to disagree with him.

4

Preparation

Irresponsible though it might seem, the plus side of driving a retired ambulance with several hundred thousand miles on the clock was that there were at least plenty of storage options.

In Audrey's belly were countless overhead cupboards and compartments that no doubt once held all sorts of life-giving drugs and equipment, but now found a new purpose as storage for our clothes, food and general supplies that would keep us alive and out of (too much) danger for the next few months.

Packing had never been a strong suit of either of ours. And that fact was especially true when the items need to be sufficiently secured to resist being jolted side to side by the harsh central Asian desert at 60 mph.

The main departments to consider were food, clothing, two beds suspended off the floor to allow us to escape the incessant sand, tools, first aid, documents, cameras, and spare fuel. All of which needed to find a home and be strapped down to stop them from rattling, breaking, smacking into one another, unscrewing themselves or leaking. We quickly learnt that if you gave anything a millimetre of wiggle room, they would find a way of opening or breaking and spilling their contents all over you and the rest of your possessions. This was especially true if they contained something especially nasty like petrol.

We fashioned a kitchen, with a gas stove, a collection of second-hand pans, crockery, and cutlery which we'd begged, borrowed, and stolen from charitable friends and family members. No matter how hard we tied them down they would rattle incessantly providing a background soundtrack to our entire journey.

Clothing choices were an interesting dilemma as we needed to cater for everything from the heat of Central Asia to the chilling cold of Siberia, the whipping sand storms of the "Stans," to the nightclubs of eastern Europe. Freddie packed especially diligently for this part of the trip. "Did I tell you it's £1 a beer in Bratislava?" he would continuously remind me.

My well-thumbed copy of *Long Way Round* by Charley Boorman and Ewan McGregor, which in retrospect inspired this journey, took a special place next to the passenger seat to provide constant inspiration for what might lay ahead.

My mother, a professional hypochondriac, also sent us packed with every possible drug and injection you could imagine. We had bandages of every description, dressings suitable for intensive surgery and enough malaria treatment to fell an elephant.

Next were the beds. We bought two camp beds made of green canvas with aluminium legs that raised us off the ground by about half a metre. Just enough to keep the sand and snakes out, we hoped.

We were locked into a game of chess with Audrey, moving pots and pans until they didn't all fall out with the mere start of her engine. When all packed and happy, we would fire her up and scream around the block, turning at the tightest possible angles left and right to road test our packing skills. Each time, pots, pans, and water bottles would fly from their previously secure places, thud into the opposite wall of the ambulance, and then crash to the floor.

The final and one of the most important areas of consideration was stash money. We had converted a serious chunk of cash into US dollars for bribes in denominations ranging from one dollar to one hundred, which was stashed under the passenger's chair under a false floor.

We stepped back to admire our work. Finally, after several days of trying and failing, everything found its place, and we were good to go. Audrey looked like a loaded wheelbarrow and cornered like it as well. Careful focus was needed around roundabouts.

The thing we didn't realise was that the twists and turns of Hampshire's laneways were no match for the never-ending rattle of a hard-baked desert track, the vibrations of which would rattle and unscrew and break anything in its deadly reach.

We probably had vastly overpacked in unnecessary areas and under-packed in vital ones. But we didn't really care. It was pretty thrilling to have everything we could need for three months — no matter what hit us — in the back of one van. It gave us a feeling of complete freedom. We could go anywhere.

* * *

Audrey wasn't the only woman we had to get ready for our trip. In the two weeks before we set off, each of our mum's made it their life's mission to imagine every possible negative scenario. And to relate these back to us. Both Freddie and I would receive frantic texts in the dead of the night, recounting nightmares of snake bites and tiger attacks. We dutifully read their pages upon pages of recommended actions should we meet one of these beasts.

Of course, some of their concerns were valid. We were to potentially face a myriad of dangers on our route. But we were embracing the spirit of adventure, not getting caught up in the what-ifs. No matter how many reams of paper our mothers printed off from the Foreign Travel Advice section of the government website, it was not going to stop us.

We could sit down and think through all the dreadful scenarios we could possibly face. But realistically, that would scare us to the point of cancelling the whole endeavour. The beauty of the trip, arguably the whole point of it, was not knowing what would happen. If we wanted anything less, we could have joined our friends in the south of France.

Nevertheless, in an effort to soothe our mother's already frayed nerves (and God knows they were to be frayed some more) we collected information about road conditions in the Balkans, the weather in northern Turkey and rudimentary Russian phrases.

* * *

Freddie's dad wisely suggested that if we were going to cross some of the most dangerous countries on earth, we better speak with someone with experience. So, he called up the local army barracks and asked if we could go down for a chat. Surprisingly, or perhaps realising that it would likely be them who would have to haul us out of a terrorist's cave kicking and screaming, they kindly agreed.

I arrived with some trepidation. I have never liked the idea of the army since being forced to join the local cadets aged thirteen and spending the next God-knows-how- many weekends in a rain-soaked ditch in Wales being shot at by "blanks" and crying for my mummy. To make matters worse, I never got along with anyone from the army, usually because they had a habit of calling me "civilian", which irks me beyond belief.

Anyway, when we arrived all my fears were proven to be absolutely correct. I got out of the car to find a six-foot-six tall brick wall of a man standing in front of me, with manicured hair, a moulded beret, and boots so clean his ego reflected back at him.

"You're late," he barked with his arms on his hips. I have to admit I didn't realise we had agreed on a time.

"You're the two planning on driving to Beijing in an ambulance?" He sneered, looking us over, inspecting our long hair, t-shirts, and flip-flops.

"Yep, that's us," I replied, trying to match his demeanour by puffing out my chest. I prepared myself for the barrage of, "You won't make it out alive, you irresponsible idiots," but he didn't need to; he said it all in one gaze.

He then gave us a rundown of what to expect. Fortunately, I could only understand one word in thirty. He barked in a constant stream of acronyms that would have challenged the most academically minded, but the two dyslexics standing in front of him just stared blankly back.

Sensing this, he delegated, "Anyway, Corporal Fisher will talk you through the basics." And with that, he turned on his heel and left.

Fortunately, Corporal Fisher was a wonderful man, in contrast. "Hello chaps, one hell of a trip you've got planned."

"We certainly hope so", we replied.

"Well, we had a few spare ration packs left over that we thought would come in handy in case the local shops were closed," he said with a smile. Maybe all army men aren't that bad after all.

"That's very kind of you, thank you!" I picked up a selection of the packs. Lamb Korma and spaghetti Bolognese, I shuddered as memories came flooding back from army cadet exercises.

"Now, talk me through your route."

We walked him through our planned list of countries, focusing especially on the juicy bits in Central Asia, which seemed to excite him the most as he bounced on the ball of his feet with the mention of the "Stans".

"Now look here, chaps. You should really be keeping your wits about you from Istanbul onwards. But especially Turkmenistan and Uzbekistan. They both share a border with Afghanistan, which, as you know, we're currently at war with."

"Yes, our parents had brought that up once or twice."

"The thing is, those borders are tremendously fluid. Some areas have limited physical separation between the countries, and as such, we often get reports of the Taliban fleeing over the border."

Well, this was new information. "there were Taliban in

Uzbekistan and Turkmenistan?" I asked.

"Most likely. In actual fact, Uzbekistan has its own branch of Al Qaeda called the IMU, the Islamic Movement of Uzbekistan, which was bankrolled by Osama Bin Laden."

"Crikey," I looked at Freddie as his eyes widened. "What are your sleeping arrangements?" he asked. "Well, erm, we haven't discussed that in a lot of detail."

"Okay, well, let me give you some pointers. With your British number plate and, how do I say this, not exactly inconspicuous, choice of vehicle. You will be a target." He said that final sentence so matter-of-factly it didn't immediately register. Freddie and I stared at him blankly, have we bitten off more than we can chew? "An attack will most likely come at night after they've been tailing you during the day."

Gulp.

"Here's what you should do. The landscape out there is mostly desert, so it's damn easy to be seen. There's very little cover. At the end of each day, before it gets dark, turn off the road at a right angle and drive straight into the desert, don't hang around. Once you've driven for about a kilometre, stop, turn around and turn off the engine. Then wait and watch to see if anyone is following you. It will be very easy to spot them when they follow you as the desert creates a cloud of dust behind anything that moves." The way he used the word "when" in that sentence unnerved me.

He continued in his 'rat-a-tat' style. "Stay there for thirty minutes at least. If nothing happens, take another right angle and drive for a further kilometre. If it's getting dark, make sure you've got your lights off. Then turn around again and watch your tracks for another thirty minutes. If again nothing happens, find a spot away from your tracks and camp up."

"And what shall we do if someone is following us?" I replied, meekly.

"Drive like hell!"

"Right boys, I need to get going. The very best of luck. I'll be cheering you on." And with that, he was gone.

I turned to Freddie as he turned to me.

"That all sounded a little real, didn't it?" I asked.

I was in two minds with all this planning and pontificating. Although relatively speaking, few travel to central Asia, a lot still do. And the vast majority of them do so without a scratch or a story to tell. If there were nasty men on their route, they let them pass through. But here's the thing, attacks do happen, and although rare, one would be enough.

"Well, we can't exactly back out now, can we? We've just spent £2,100 on a fucking ambulance." Freddie summarised with a shrug.

* * *

During all of this preparation and rigorous testing, we managed to attract some press attention. Whilst it wasn't quite *The Times* and *the Telegraph*, we had promised our dear sponsors, but we did receive glowing coverage in the Cotswold Journal, with a circulation of around thirteen plus a dog and a duck, and the

Oxford Times. "See, I told you we'd get in the Times," I said to my uncle with more than a dollop of guilt. We took what we got.

The final job on our to-do list was organising our triumphant departure: ticker-tape parade, waving friends and family, like old explorers going off into the new world, we thought.

We had arranged a big send-off at a friend's house. A marquee was erected, kegs of beer bought, shrieking fans installed, you get the picture. We planned to arrive fashionably late when everyone else was settled into a few drinks, and the merriment had begun; we would turn up with shrieking sirens, flashing lights and loud cheering from the fans. It was going to be quite the sight.

We planned it perfectly; we knew exactly when to leave to arrive at the right moment. The time came; we strapped ourselves in and set off to our party.

"We're a bit low on fuel," I turned to Freddie.

"We don't have time; we'll fill up tomorrow," he replied.

"Are you sure? I'm not sure how long the fuel light has been on." "We're already late!"

Two miles from the party, I felt the pressure of the accelerator give way. I pumped my foot, but there was no resistance. Audrey started to decelerate.

"What were you doing?" Asked Freddie. "I think we're out of fuel, mate," I replied.

"Stop fucking around; come on, let's get there." "I really wish I was, mate."

She crawled down to 10mph and then freewheeled. "Quick, pull in."

I pulled the steering wheel, and Audrey crawled into the lay-by. And then choked as her engine stalled. I tried to restart the engine but just got a mechanical click, click, click in reply.

"Well, this was fucking embarrassing," I said as I rested my head on the wheel in frustration.

We had only planned to drive Audrey to our party and then to Dover, so we hadn't bothered to buy roadside cover in the UK.

I grimaced as the kind man at AA quoted the cost of a litre of fuel getting dropped at our location. A few beers and meals struck off our budget.

We eventually arrived two hours late. The news of our shortcoming had already trickled around the party. We arrived to jeers and laughter rather than the hero's welcome we had envisioned.

"The only way that ambulance was making it to Beijing is in a fucking box!" shouted one reveller. Where had I heard that before?

* * *

Look, I know what you're thinking. I'm with you.

Our preparations for the trip might come across as haphazard, even irresponsible. But, looking back on them now, I think there was something a little deeper than that.

Freddie and I had come to fear the structured life that lay ahead of us. The way life is painted out for you before you've even begun like a blueprint, just waiting for your first foot to land on step one, and then you're whisked away on the escalator of tedium.

I think that's what drove our decision in the first place.

Neatly skipping from university to the corporate world felt like we were placing our foot on that slow escalator known as growing up.

Our refusal to properly plan anything or, for that matter, take anything very seriously was all part of that. We were in that heady adolescent mindset of buying the ticket and taking the ride. Of setbacks being life lessons and nothing more.

In any case, life is more fun if you treat it as a series of impulses.

Our lack of visas or equipment and attempting the trip with a hopelessly unsuitable vehicle and a fist full of maps was our way of showing the world it could be done, without following your rules.

It was going to be a journey of a lifetime. We were going to trace the footsteps of the great explorers, travellers, and merchants from west to east and do it all, laughably, in an ambulance from Manchester called Audrey.

Everyone, to a man, advised us against it. They said such things as, "You should be focusing on getting work experience..."

"Work experience" — is there a worse phrase in the English language? If I wanted to experience work, why wouldn't I find work that actually paid? I did try work experience once, the summer prior. I spent £100 on a suit, bought with great ceremony as it was my "first suit", to spend the week photocopying and pressing buttons on a coffee machine. If that was an accurate "experience" of what office working life was like, we shouldn't encourage young people to extend the portion of their life given to it. Particularly as it's unpaid and there's so much of the world to see.

Anyway, let's begin.

5

Europe

On the big day, just a few weeks after we had come up with this ridiculous idea, I arrived at Freddie's house for our grand departure. It was a beautiful English summer's day, the beer gardens were ready to be filled up, the barbecues were being lit, and the Pimm's was waiting to be poured. The fact they come along so rarely makes you appreciate them all the more, don't you think? I was full of the buzzed excitement, anticipation and nervousness that precedes any big trip.

I knocked on the front door after, quite literally, skipping down the garden path. And after a concerning delay, I knocked again. He couldn't have forgotten? Or God forbid, talked himself out of the trip during a restless night of the soul?

After a third knock, the door creaked open and a face emerged shielding itself from the bright light of the day with one hand. Freddie stood before me still in his Pyjamas and wrapped in a duvet.

"I'm guessing you haven't packed?" I said with more than a hint of sarcasm. "Sorry mate, big night."

Freddie, on the eve of the biggest trip of our lifetime, had spent the evening gazing at the bottom of a bottle.

I pushed him into the shower, flicked on the kettle and reluctantly took responsibility for throwing the clothes I could find into the back of the van.

Freddie emerged twenty minutes later with one eye open, still swaying from side to side, saying something about his shirt. I thrust a cup of coffee into his quivering hands and threw him into the passenger seat.

I walked around the back of Audrey and jumped in myself.

I looked over, Fred was already lying motionless with his head against the window. I gave the siren a short shriek which jolted him upright, and made me chuckle. One – nil.

I put Audrey into first, released the clutch and gently pressed down on the accelerator. We crawled out of the driveway and turned right. And just like that, as casually as a Monday morning commute, we were off.

Our goal for day one was to reach Cologne, just over the German border where our friend Mark was waiting for us. Contrary to our previous unsuccessful persuasions, Mark had agreed to join us through Europe "and no fucking further." His aim for the trip was resolutely driven by beer and the girls of Eastern Europe and he made no excuses or secret of the matter.

We headed southeast to Dover where a ferry would take us to France. I left Freddie to his slumber and lost myself in my own thoughts. We passed countless BMWs and Mercedes rushing into London on their commute. Glum faces stuck to coffee mugs and mobile telephones. Sensible people with steady jobs. Were we the mad ones, or were they?

We arrived at Dover to a throng of activity and commerce. Lorries lined up to serve all corners of the earth, and families standing leaning against their cars waiting for their vessel. We paid our dues and, after a short wait, boarded the ferry, parked Audrey down below, and headed up to the top deck.

"Coffee," Freddie muttered as he felt the magnetic pull of the cafe.

I headed to the top deck. Strangely it was here, as I gazed across the English Channel, that the nerves hit. But they weren't due to the very real dangers we might face over the next three months; the fear was more profound than that — it was a fear of failure. This was a journey of a lifetime, one that countless armchair travellers dream of but never take, and this was our opportunity, our one opportunity to do it justice.

Arriving back home with Audrey in a box was a mental image that kept me awake at night. We couldn't fail. So many people had told us that we were mad even to try. If we failed, it would teach us that we couldn't swim against the tide. It would teach us to get back in our box and buckle up.

Looking back, it was an achievement just to be on that ferry, to even stand a chance of getting to Beijing, to have made it off the start line. Ever since that first day in Oxford when we pitched our grand plan to our housemates, we'd been met by derision every step of the way. "That's the stupidest thing I've ever heard," which put out our backs and doubled down our stubbornness. I think if anyone had said, "Good idea, I'm coming," on that first day, we would never have made it on the ferry.

Poor Freddie spent the journey spitting his breakfast over the railings whilst making strange heaving noises.

A man from a speaker told us it was time to head back down and after a short wait, we were released from the belly of the beast and were spilt into France like marauding ants. We immediately took a left turn and headed east. A trajectory we would follow until we hit Beijing.

It should be said, I love Europe. I love how at the same time we're all so similar: we all love football, live in small houses in ancient cities and are liberally minded, yet so different. The food, the language and everyday customs change after just the briefest of drives. Germany and France share borders, but culturally they are from the opposite ends of the earth.

I love Europe's glorious unpredictability and love the fact that its citizens make no excuse for it. I've subsequently lived in America, which was both built for the modern world. As practical as it is boring. Give me a narrow, cobbled street built for the horse and carriage, lined with *alfresco* diners and aggressive waiters to drive down over a zippy freeway any day of the week.

We pressed on towards Germany after leaving France behind and headed into Belgium. Driving through the industrial suburbs of northern Europe, the workhorse that pays for the playground of its southern neighbours.

For the first time, we got a chance to see what Audrey was made of. How much of her old turn of foot did she have? After all, speed is a valuable asset in the emergency world.

I advanced through the gears whilst pressing my foot to the floor. Up into 3rd. The car ahead grew larger in our windshield. Time to make a move and claim our first victim of the tour. I pulled out into the overtaking lane and slid her into 4th. I released the clutch and pressed my foot back to the floor, expecting to be pushed back into my seat as we sailed past our competitor. But nothing. No acceleration. I pumped my foot. I even leaned forward. But she wouldn't budge above 40mph. The poor girl has the aerodynamics of a brick, and bringing her out of the slipstream almost put her into reverse.

I shamefully admitted defeat and pulled back into the slow lane after some aggressive honking and flashing from behind.

This trip might take longer than I thought.

When we hit the outskirts of Brussels, I shook Freddie awake. I'd had enough of my own company for one day. In any case, I needed a map reader.

In an act of great ceremony, he unsheathed the first of our Stanford maps, which covered Western Europe. He opened it up like a broadsheet paper, causing me to lose all view of the road ahead. I wrestled it away just in time to watch Audrey scatter a flock of elderly pedestrians off the road ahead.

Freddie confidently, but quite wrongly, directed me off the ring road into the centre of Brussels to "have a look around", he later told me, barely managing to shield his embarrassment.

Brussels was an odd place to an Englishman. To some of our more excitable politicians, it has come to represent everything that was wrong and evil about mankind. The mere mention of the word in certain parts of the country can cause a previously mild-mannered family man to combust into fits of rage and finger-pointing. "The bureaucracy!" they shout. "The unelected politicians!" they bemoan. "They are nothing but rats in suits!" Okay, maybe I made that last one up, but the sentiment is there. So much so that I half expected to see thousands upon thousands of shifty-looking men in suits drowning themselves in champagne, gorging on lobster, and paying on a credit card emblazoned with "UK Government."

But alas, everyone seemed to be going about their business in a diligent manner in a town like any other in Europe. Shamefully, I was a little disappointed, I wanted to see this reckless excess for myself and perhaps join in. Then at least we'd be getting our money's worth.

Disillusioned, we pressed on through the rush hour traffic, looking for signs to the German border.

If you blink at the wrong moment, you can cross European borders without realising. Suddenly all the road signs changed in tone from the mild-mannered suggestions of Belgium to the fierce, upon pain of death, instructions of Germany. Full of exclamation marks and "*Achtung!*" They do love an exclamation mark in Germany. But then again, anything in German makes me jump out of my seat as if I've just been caught smoking by the headmaster. Do you know what the German for daisy is? Possibly the sweetest sounding word in the English language is translated as Gänseblümchen or as it sounds in my head: GANSEBLUMCHEN!!!!

I motored on, trying not to take offence from the road signs.

As we drew near Cologne, my thirst increased, hoping Mark was by now well versed as to the whereabouts of the top beer houses. Mark was a friend from university and, in the context of our friends at University, quite a smart one. We had all spent three years together at Oxford Brookes which is kindly known as "the early learning centre" by the students at the more famous and intellectual neighbouring university. Freddie and I studied property, of which the sum total of my learnings could be extensively written out on a postage stamp, whereas Mark had studied finance, which sounded much more serious and intellectually stimulating. Mark had always claimed he clicked on the wrong Oxford when applying. I'm not sure I believe that, but his presence there was an oddity.

It probably shouldn't have come as much of a surprise to us

when he wanted to spend a summer blowing off some steam after three years being taught how to count to ten. Mark was also South African by birth and upbringing and, as such had some catching up to in ticking off European countries. It was good to have him on board.

Mark had locked us down a parking space which, as I reversed into, caused me to realise something that shouldn't have been a realisation. She's a devil to park, Audrey. For some reason, ambulance manufacturers provide you with a perfectly good rear view mirror, clearly forgetting that you have a one-tonne box on the back. That is, I shouldn't have to say, not transparent. By looking into the rear-view mirror all you can see is the backboard of the cabin two inches from your head. I couldn't shake the habit of putting Audrey into reverse and naturally turning my head to the rear-view mirror and then cursing the damn manufacturer for being so cruel.

Mark guided me back into the parking spot and I got out to give Mark a hug. I was glad to have some human company that was capable of more than two syllables in succession. "Take me to the nearest bar," I instructed. "Take me to my bed," Freddie mumbled. Or at least I think that was what he said, I was already halfway down the street.

Determined not to let a hangover get in the way of our first night of freedom, we found the nearest bar and sat Freddie down where we could keep a close eye on him. He has an amazing Houdini-like ability to sneak out of a bar and head home when the feeling takes him.

They've made a wonderful discovery in Cologne, and I can't think why it hasn't been adopted by the rest of the world. They drink their beer out of small glasses known as a *Stange*. Think of a glass just larger than a test tube from your chemistry class, about that size, filled with beer (Stange literally translates to 'a pole' if that helps you visualise). You can hold them between thumb and forefinger and knock them back in between two and three sips. And most notably of all, the barmaids work on an opt-out basis. That is they will continue to replenish your Stange, mostly when you are not looking, until you explicitly tell them not to. A lot of thought has gone into drinking efficiency in this country, and God bless them for it. And they really do knock them back at freighting speed. Within minutes your concerns are no longer, and you are friends with half the bar.

To start with we sat in silence, consumed with this new and novel way of drinking. But soon enough one leg started jigging up and down involuntarily, and then the other. I then became full of all the joys of adventure and bored anyone unlucky enough to be within earshot of the possibilities of the world and how lucky we were to live in this great and glorious time. Before I knew it, I had my arms around a local dancing to *Polka* music before being hauled to bed by Freddie and Mark, taking one side each.

I awoke the next morning to find Freddie with a smug smile on his face that told me he was going to take every opportunity to repay my cruelty from yesterday.

"Count your lucky stars you don't have to get on a fucking ferry, mate," Freddie began.

"Coffee!" I blurted in reply whilst holding my forehead and grasping for nothing in particular.

We burst out into the morning sunshine, leaving me grappling for my sunglasses. As we walked down the street in search of breakfast, I was amazed to find the Germans still drinking. Table after table after table had beers perched atop, glinting in the morning sun. Sturdy Germans sat behind them eating their breakfast, not in the least bit ashamed or embarrassed by this activity.

The only difference between a German and an alcoholic is that a German has his morning beer with a pretzel and a sausage.

The plan for the day was to head south-east from Cologne past Frankfurt to the forests outside of Nuremberg to put us in striking distance of the Czech Republic the following day. Mark chucked his rucksack into the van and jumped in for our first drive together. There was only room for one passenger in the front, so we'd rotate through the van, one person sitting in the paramedic's chair in the back. Whether that was a curse or a blessing depended on your state of mind at the time. The position of the "third man" as we came to call it was originally in one of the camp beds, but after sustaining serious bruising from being flipped out as Freddie took a roundabout at speed, I took the sensible decision to sit in the paramedic's seat, which at least had a seatbelt.

The day gave us the opportunity to introduce Audrey to the speed-limitless *Autobahn*. Full of crazy Germans travelling at breakneck speeds. Every country seems to have one law that makes absolutely no sense to the outside world, the Americans have their guns, and in Germany, they have their speed limits or lack thereof.

Audrey, as you might suspect already, was no match for the speeding BMWs and Audis with their matching bald-headed drivers whizzing past her outside. There seemed to be a direct correlation between lack of hair and speed. Probably penis size as well. It seemed unlikely these men had anywhere to get to in their great rush.

We arrived at the forests outside of Nuremberg in the early afternoon and were greeted by spectacular rising peaks covered in dense forestland and rushing rivers. It looked like something straight out of *Hansel and Gretel.* Having never been to Germany before, we realised we had hugely underrated the country's natural beauty.

When choosing a holiday in Europe, most flock to the beaches of Spain, the cities of France or the restaurants of Italy. But never Germany; why is that? Perhaps a hangover from the war. I remember when I was younger, my parents bought a Bosch washing machine, and in protest, my grandmother didn't speak to us for a year. God knows what she would have thought of me now being behind enemy lines. After all, they went through, it's difficult to blame her generation for their views, and I wonder how much has subconsciously dripped down to my parents and indeed to me.

We soon turned off onto a back road to find a spot to camp and found a clearing in the forest next to an old Bavarian castle. As the sun descended, the dying light turned the castle from a marvel of Bavarian architecture to Dracula's lair as the moonlight flickered on its walls.

We made the necessary arrangements to set up camp and then sat back to enjoy our first-night camping outside. It really felt like that now the game was afoot. Our first night in Cologne was great to blow off the cobwebs but not a unique experience. But now that we were camping, it really felt like the adventure had started.

We built a large campfire and then did what any Englishman would do in such a situation: draw some stumps on the back of Audrey and have a good game of cricket, much to the bemusement of the few Germans who happened to walk past.

As Mark was only joining us to Istanbul "and no fucking further!," the sleeping situation had not really been designed with him in mind, with just the two camp beds. But we had packed a particularly unsteady hammock that would swing from the rooftop.

As such, the cricket suddenly took on a lot more significance to us three as it became the nightly decider of who would sleep in the hammock. On that first night, as Freddie came around the wicket delivering impossible to play leg-spin (more by accident than skill) Mark's poor shot selection resigned him to an equally poor night's sleep in the hammock after nicking it to slip.

We then spent an enjoyable half-hour watching Mark trying to wrestle his way into his hammock. Each doomed attempt mostly involved sharp intakes of breath, followed by bending of the knees, a big jump, legs kicking fresh air as he landed on his stomach, a second of balance where we'd think he'd finally made it, before being catapulted out the other side. He then switched to the jumping-in-arse-first technique and then resigned himself to the belly flop approach, arms outstretched to ensure greater surface area. Freddie and I laid on our backs, hands tucked behind our heads, as he resembled a novice surfer trying to drag his body upwards before a lack of balance sent him crashing back to the floor. But now he was just inviting Freddie and I to go fuck ourselves whilst we couldn't contain our giggles.

That morning Freddie and I woke early to the sounds of Mark stumbling around the campsite looking for coffee and grumbling about his poor night's sleep.

We packed up and continued our journey east to the Czech

border. The Germans have built an incredibly fast and efficient motorway network which spares any sort of visual stimulation, so I'll save your boredom and refrain from further description.

We stopped for lunch in an old medieval town just outside Nuremberg called Bamberg for our final set of German sausages. In German restaurants you were either offered sausages or knuckle, god knows what they do with the rest of the poor animal, but we stuck to the sausages and became strangely attached.

We circled the town looking for a place to park. I was driving, with Mark in the passenger seat and Freddie swinging around in the hammock in the back, still unable to shake his now three-day hangover.

We spotted an underground car park and headed down the slope to the entrance. Not knowing exactly how tall Audrey was, I asked Mark to get out and assess our chances of making it underneath the barrier.

"Yeah, should be fine, mate, plenty of room" he replied.

Happy with the confident tone of Mark's response, I released the brake and Audrey started picking up speed. As we reached the bottom of the slope, Audrey stopped dead in her tracks, throwing us forward in our seats, our chests smacking against our seatbelts. Accompanied by an almighty crack of fibreglass breaking overhead.

Followed almost immediately by a bemused Freddie bellowing, "Max! What the fuck have you done?" As he struggled to escape his hammock. It was the first we'd heard of him all morning.

I held my breath, an awful feeling in my stomach as I got out to assess the damage. Mark stayed precisely where he was, staring ahead as if he couldn't believe his calculations were so far off. Maybe he was right for Oxford Brookes after all.

From standing on her front wheel, I could see that Mark's calculations hadn't even been close. Audrey's fibreglass roof had comfortably smashed into the underside of the carpark roof about halfway along. There was a vast indentation in the fibreglass and concerning-looking cracks spreading out in all directions. It looked like she had nearly been split in half.

"Ah, it doesn't look too bad," I shouted with complete false hope.

Freddie, who was making a huge amount of noise trying to escape his hammock and exit the van, eventually made it out with saucepans and mugs bearing the wrath of his anger.

"Doesn't look too fucking bad!?" he shouted as he finally managed to escape the vehicle. "You've wedged us onto the fucking roof!"

Mark was keeping a low profile and trying to think of excuses.

"Well, I was nearly right," he eventually said, "We made it halfway."

A car sounded its horn behind us, and we turned to find a growing traffic jam of increasingly angry Germans behind us.

The Germans are known for many things, but patience, when blown off schedule, is certainly not one of them. At the time, I blamed their aggressive honking on this stereotype but looking back, I can see how the incident would have caused even the mildest of monks to lose his cool and lean on his car horn.

It was a one-way entrance. There was no way we could carry on — we would have to reverse. As Mark had made the fateful judgement, it was his job to explain in his best German to all the cars behind us that they would have to reverse back up the ramp and onto the street to let us get out. He came back red-faced after some colourful replies.

To add to our trouble, the security barrier had already shut behind us and was only triggered from one side. A problem for later. First, we needed to get Audrey unstuck.

I got back into the van and thrust her into reverse. I released the clutch and timidly pressed down on the accelerator; she didn't budge. I pushed further down on the throttle. Audrey screamed in protest, I could feel her whole chassis bending up and buckling against the underside of the roof with a sickening crunching noise as black smoke puffed out of the bonnet. It was useless. We were completely stuck. I released the accelerator, our local mechanic's advice before we left ringing in my ears: "Just don't burn out the clutch!"

"Please don't let our trip end like this," I muttered to myself with my head on the steering wheel. It would be so embarrassing to return home to all our "I told you so" friends having only made it to a car park in Germany.

All the borders, bandits and off-road driving we had ahead of us. We couldn't even negotiate a fucking underground car park in Bavaria.

"Why don't you try edging forward a little," said Mark. He had been keeping so quiet, his voice startled me. "How the hell would that help us?" I replied.

"Well, it might help us get unstuck. In any case, have you got a better idea?" The stress of the situation, the damaged pride, was clearly wearing on more than just me.

I really didn't.

I put her back into first and gently released the clutch.

Just at that moment, Freddie, who had been looking for help, returned with a German security guard.

"What the fuck are you doing!" He shouted down the ramp

seeing our attempt to go forward rather than back, "You're meant to be going backwards not forwards!"

Freddie develops quite a colourful vocabulary when he's stressed.

Then something gave with a crack. I quickly put her back into reverse and, ever so slowly and with a long, grinding creak and a spine-chilling scrapping noise that every bad driver knows only too well, we managed to reverse back out from under the concrete ceiling. Taking a good chunk of it with us as the smoke from Audrey's bonnet and dust from the dropping rubble enveloped us, leaving a yellow stain from Audrey's paintwork permanently scarred on the car park ceiling.

The security guard, wiping concrete dust from his uniform, then kindly opened the barrier — more than likely just glad to see the back of us — and we reversed back up the slope with all the pots and pans Freddie had kicked over in his range smashing around in the back.

We reached the top of the slope and were confronted by a huge queue of angry Germans hitting their horns and staring at us over their moustaches. "Get in, Fred!" He didn't need telling twice and jumped in the back as we sped away, swearing never to try and park anywhere with a roof ever again.

The relief we felt as we made our exit quickly vanished as smoke continued to billow from Audrey's bonnet.

We found the nearest side street, parked, and opened her up, letting out a massive plume of smoke like a small atomic mushroom cloud from her bonnet. We pulled out our water jerry cans and poured them over the engine. We had no idea if that was the right thing to do, but it seemed sensible at the time.

With the smoke dying down, we left the bonnet open and

went off to find some lunch to let the engine cool down and to regroup. A hugely needed final round of German sausage and beers were ordered.

On our return, there was no smoke, no fire, but a bright yellow parking ticket on Audrey's windscreen. Filled with rage at how wrong everything was going already, I pulled it off, tore it up and chucked it in the nearest bin.

"Good luck chasing us to fucking Beijing," I muttered to no one in particular.

And with that, I chucked the keys to Fred: "Your turn to drive," and sloped off to sleep in the back.

That was the last I saw of Germany.

6

Czech Republic

I woke up a few hours later as we were arriving in Prague with renewed positivity. The back of the van, apart from a small sliding window to the front cabin, was completely closed off to the outside. With the hammock gently rocking to the flow of Audrey's movements, you could actually get some surprisingly decent shuteye, as long as the driving was smooth which (again, surprisingly) it was for the most part. God bless those German *Autobahns*.

As we approached the city, I stuck my head through the front window which opened into the cab.

"Evening, boys!"

"Ah, Max, good you're awake," said Freddie with an unbelievably smug look on his face. "I've been waiting to tell you, Audrey hit her top speed on the Autobahn crossing the border. 65 mph!"

Fred patted Audrey on her dashboard the way a proud father would pat his child on the head. It was a good 5 mph more than I'd achieved entering Germany which irked my competitive side. I looked to Mark for corroboration. He shrugged his shoulders in a way that told me he was way above mine and Freddie's childish games.

"Well, we will have to drink to Audrey's accomplishment tonight then! God knows I need a couple," I replied.

I stayed leaning through the window to watch our arrival into Prague — a city none of us had been to before. It was spectacular driving over the bridge of the Vltava with the early evening sunlight reflecting off the Gothic architecture of the Old Town with the Prague Castle suspended in the background.

"Tonight's going to be a good night, I think."

Many travel Europe by rail, which must be a breeze arriving at a new city each day with nothing but a backpack and anticipation. However, our arrival in each city would be beset by the stress of tiny laneways, one-way streets and micro-sized parking spaces. As you doubtless know, the Europeans drive Mickey Mouse cars, all of them. And the parking spaces were designed as such. I don't blame them, if I had to drive down a street purposely designed to remove wing mirrors, I'd do the same. But this meant that we had to find two adjoining parking spaces for Audrey each night. It was the vehicular equivalent of shopping at High and Mighty. And as my 6ft8 uncle will tell you, there ain't one on every street. And as I will now tell you, there ain't one in every town, either. We'd often have to resort to parking in nearby towns and villages and then catching a taxi to our intended location, being careful to remember the name of the town we parked in.

And so we began our nightly search for two free adjoining parking spaces. We'd long given up on maintaining any semblance of paint work on Audrey's flanks as restaurant tables and their accompanying diners, traffic wardens and tour guides would scrape her clean as we squeezed down narrow alleyways. Unfortunately, our Stanford's European maps would abandon us as we entered cities. "You're on your own from here, mate," they'd cry, and leave us with a brown smudge that represented the entirety of Prague. On two separate occasions, we found the needle in the haystack only for the rear of the two spaces to be snatched away by a dexterous granny in a Volkswagen Beetle. Finally, accompanied by the kind of sweats and longing that only beset someone who long ago promised himself a crisp beer, we found a parking space in a nearby country.

We packed up a bag each, left Audrey to her own devices for the evening and set off heads down arms pumping in search of a hostel for the night. We didn't have a long list of requirements, "As long as I'm not sleeping in a fucking swing again, I'm happy" was Mark's input, and as such we quickly found a few beds in a shared dorm near the central station. After a quick shower and a change of clothes, we headed out. The hostel only gave us one key between the three of us, which, for reasons unfathomable, we gave to Freddie to look after.

After a restorative meal of roast pork and dumplings with sauerkraut, which was better than it sounded, and a number of beers, we headed to one of Prague's more infamous landmarks, a huge five-storey nightclub that boasts of being the largest in central Europe. It heralds a level of infamy that dictates it's the first question you ask, or are asked, if someone tells you or you tell someone you are headed to Prague. The number of doubtless made-up stories we heard of the place put it on a level with the full moon party in Thailand. The concept of the club was simple, if you get bored of the music, you simply change floors. Whether you were into the Beatles, Bob Marley, or Bach (Okay, maybe not Bach), there was a floor for you.

Being a group of three men, we queued until the birds started chirping and then paid the monthly wage of an honest labourer to gain entry, upon which we immediately lost each other. Freddie, probably relishing the opportunity to spend some time with members of his own musical taste, rushed off to find a room full of 75-year-old white men. Whereas I entertained myself on the chill floor, where I spent the night chatting happily with strangers of all nationalities with a soft backdrop of electronic music. I've long learnt that if I want to have any chance of success in a nightclub, it's best to keep off the dance floor. I was filled with the friendlessness you only get in foreign and exciting cities, I circulated like I was at a cocktail party, meeting more people in an hour than I'd met in Oxford in a year. I bought drinks for every stranger in the bar, several times over. I laughed uncontrollably at any and every story told to me and generally fell in love with everyone that I met, boy or girl. And just as I was finding my groove, that happy balance when social confidence is sky-high, yet basic coordination is still assured, the lights came on. Blinding me and stopping me in full flow just as I was reaching the punchline of a story I'd told many times over to the same group of people who stood before me. It was like being woken up in the middle of a really good dream.

I shielded my eyes and stumbled around the club, looking for Freddie and Mark. The previously cool and classy interior looked tacky and tasteless in that eastern European sort of way, now it was bathed in the harshness of neon light.

I found Mark sitting in a corner, looking despondent. "No luck, mate?" I asked, already knowing the answer.

"I got so close," he replied, "Then her friend got too drunk, and she had to take her home."

"Happens to the best of us, mate," I said as I pulled him up

69

and propped his armpit onto of my shoulder. "Let's get you to bed, now, where is Fred?"

"I saw him talking with an Aussie girl."

I sighed; I knew from bitter experience not to expect a cursory "I'm heading back" text from Freddie. He notoriously conducts his dating work with utmost secrecy.

"Oh well, we'll catch him in the morning," I said.

"What. A. Night," I said to Mark as we meandered back towards our hostel in a perfect warm and starry night, ignoring the typical scenes of debauchery found on European streets at such an hour. Stag parties searching for lost comrades, sobbing teenage girls with mascara-scarred faces being chased by apologetic boys of a similar age, various stages of the walking wounded limping or being carried home.

We got to the front door of our hostel and I turned expectantly to Mark. He looked back at me blankly.

"Well, come on then. Open the door." I pressed down on the handle to make my point.

"I hav..."

"Oh, fuck," I realised. "Freddie!" I screamed into the night sky like a howling wolf and kicked the ground in frustration.

I sat down and pulled out my phone. Twenty missed calls later, Freddie still had the keys. Suddenly Prague had lost its charm. A wind had come, and the warm and beautiful night now had a chill to it.

I stood up to try and search for a bell and came face to face with a sign that said, "If you're locked out, you're locked out!" Hospitality at its finest.

"Well, I guess this is us for the night," I said to Mark. After his near-miss at the bar, Mark was already in a considerably worse mood than me, even before this realisation, so this just pushed him further into his gloom.

At least it's dry, I thought as I placed my head on the doorstep and tried to get comfortable. Mark curled up with his head on my legs and made his frustrations clear through some loud grunting and groaning. Not the kind of *alfresco* sleeping I had in mind for this trip.

We woke up at 4.30 am to Freddie returning — kicked out for poor performance, I suspected.

"What on earth are you boys doing out here?" He shouted as he kicked us awake.

"What the fuck do you think? You've got the fucking keys, and we called you about twenty times!" I shouted. Mark was too angry to say anything. The poor man had had a rough night.

"I don't know what you're talking about," Freddie replied.

And with that, he nonchalantly unlocked the door, headed up to our room and fell asleep without another word.

The plan the next morning was to get up early to cross the Austrian border and head to Vienna. But the previous night's activities meant we were all nursing heavy hangovers and weren't exactly on speaking terms, so we didn't leave till early afternoon.

We finally managed to pull ourselves together enough to face another day's hard- driving. Through guilt, although there was never an official apology, Fred offered to drive. Mark, who still couldn't bring himself to speak to Freddie, fell into the hammock in the back, and there he stayed. I think poor old Mark had felt that a part of his manhood had been irreparably damaged by spending the night on the street and wasn't taking the hit to his ego well. Far from my first night on the streets, I was largely over the matter. But I was determined not to let Freddie get away with it lightly and so slumped into the passenger seat and pretended to sleep, letting Freddie drive all the way to Austria and map read and refuel, twice. *That should teach him,* I thought (God, I can be petty on little sleep).

Growing up I had the dubious honour of being the most dyslexic boy in the whole of South West England (and as my editor can attest, I'm still up there). So much so that I could never tell the difference between Austria and Australia. Which caused much confusion and embarrassment when I arrived at the Austrian border aged ten for a family holiday and demanded to see their finest kangaroos, immediately. This time I intended to make a better impression.

Shortly after crossing the border, we admitted defeat realising that we had no chance of making Vienna before nightfall and camped beside a beautiful lake with just the hint of the Austrian Alps as a backdrop. Our fellow campers' initial alarm when they saw an ambulance slowly making its way across the field towards them, turned into complete confusion when we got out and started making arrangements for camp. "English," I heard someone in our neighbouring camp say, with raised eyebrows in a way that suggested that explained everything.

Freddie made a last-ditch attempt to get back into our good books by trying to catch a fish for dinner with the rod we'd packed. I had seen a sign that said "no fish" on the way in, but I enjoyed watching him swat the water madly for two hours — I even let Mark into my little joke, which brought him out of his gloom with a smile.

Hungry, with the light waning, we resigned ourselves to heating up the first of our army ration bags. I had chicken curry, which tasted neither of chicken nor curry. I really appreciate all the army did for us, but when you eat something that bad, it never leaves you. I can taste it to this day.

We lit a bonfire by the lake and listened to music as we washed away the foul-tasting rations and the worries of the previous day with the last of our German beer. All was right in the world again. Freddie had clambered back into our good books. We never did learn why he was kicked out at four am.

We woke up to an amazing sunrise over the lake. It was early summer and hot. In such conditions, Audrey acted as a greenhouse on wheels. Each morning we only had about forty-five minutes from sunrise until it was completely insufferable to be in the back. One of us would have to burst the back doors open to let in some cool breeze and let the stench escape.

We got up and cooled off with a swim in the lake. I lay on my back in the water, gazing up at the sky. The lake fed off Alpine glaziers thousands of metres above us and was frighteningly cold. But something about cold water swimming revives the spirit and sends my mood sky-high.

"Hey, Freddie," I shouted, "After Istanbul, no more hostels, let's camp every night." "I'm in," he replied.

After cooking a hearty breakfast, we cracked on. Reluctantly we skipped Vienna, we had to get Mark to Istanbul for his flight home in time for his new job, and we had no idea what the roads would be like in Romania and Bulgaria.

We crossed through Austria that morning, just clipping the edge of it in a matter of hours. All we saw of the country was its low-lying agricultural area, full of cornfields and busy-looking farmers pulling vast machinery behind tractors. The alps teased us to our right, far in the distance. Going all the way to Austria and not going to the Alps or Vienna was like flying to Disneyland just to use their facilities. But needs must.

We'll get you next time, I thought.

For the last hundred Austrian kilometres, we joined the Danube, which became a good friend. We would follow it all the way to our next destination, Bratislava, and then on to Budapest, and through Romania to the Black Sea. Consulting my guidebook, I learned that the Danube passes through more countries than any other river in the world. Well, there you go.

Crossing the Slovakian border, we headed straight for the capital, Bratislava. After travelling through the medieval and imperial beauty of much of Europe, the architecture of Eastern Europe hits you like a slap in the face. As we approached, the brutalist apartment blocks rose before us. Like an unshakable hangover from Soviet times, the city was scarred by these concrete-ridden buildings, oppressive in their size and uniformity. You know when you're entering the old Soviet empire when you start seeing little old men hunched over chess tables surrounded by other little old men passing out advice. Isn't it interesting that the Soviet empire only lasted 69 years, a shorter lifespan than the average person, yet it had such a cultural impact on those within its grasp? There's nothing as strong as a shared belief. Vienna to Bratislava takes just over an hour to drive, yet you feel like you've gone back decades.

The people changed too. Austria is the last staging post of Westernism in all its forms. The fashion, music, and optimism change as you cross the border. You immediately get the sense that people aren't on the same wavelength as you anymore.

There were a couple of major reasons we had chosen Bratislava on our route. According to our guidebook, Bratislava contains the highest number of beautiful women *per capita* anywhere in the world. Freddie had found this fact halfway across the English Channel and jumped to his feet with the discovery. "Max, look at this." How they measure this fact, I do not know, but we'll take it.

Secondly, the Slovakians love their booze. They were ranked in the top ten heaviest drinkers on the planet, with each person gulping down the equivalent of thirteen litres of pure alcohol each year. That's 1,300 shots of Jack Daniels a year. Four shots a day with no days off!

The combination sounded like a potent mix. We arrived, found a hostel, and then spent the afternoon lying by the Danube in the sun — which was pretty idyllic.

The rest of the night proceeded as any night would proceed when the beer costs $1 a litre. It was the type of city that didn't wait for you to order a beer. Waitresses thrust it upon you as soon as you'd finished your previous. And usually not thrust into your hand, but straight down your throat. If you so wished, there was no need to leave your seat all evening, which, combined with the cheap beer, was a dangerous cocktail.

The waitresses set a blistering pace, beer after beer was slapped down on the table barely before you'd finished your last. They'd watch you like hawks for any sign of a final sip.

Clearly bored with my current company, I spent much of the evening offering lifts to Bulgaria and beyond to anyone that would listen. Unsurprisingly, only one person accepted, Naoki, a mechanic from Japan — the perfect complement to our completely non-existent mechanical skillset. *I must tell the others*, I thought. I made many other friends that night. I talked to people from all four corners of the world and from every profession known to man. What I talked to them about is anyone's guess, but I certainly don't remember being stuck for words.

When all was said and done, we attempted to meander back to our hostel. Halfway back, Mark interrupted our mindless drivel by barking, "Quick, put your wallet in your pants."

"What were you talking about, Mark?" we both replied, dismissing his beer talk.

As soon as the words had left my mouth, I felt a blow from behind to the right side of my face, knocking me to the floor. I looked back up, holding my stinging face with ringing in my ears, to see a Bratislavan man the size of a fridge standing over me. He looked down on me with a clenched jaw, narrow eyes, and a still fisted hand, his shirt tight against his bulging chest and biceps. He wasn't just letting off steam after a long week; there was vivid anger in his eyes.

Happy with his night's work, he dismissed me on the floor and moved on to Mark, grabbing onto his t-shirt with one hand and punching him in the face with the other.

His friend, meanwhile, who was of similar proportions and motives, began to set upon Freddie and me. Being the hardened fighters we are, we ran to the nearest bit of cover we could find, a bus shelter. And then (which must have been comical to anyone watching but was definitely not to us), we began a weird dance with our assailant, with him on one side of the bus shelter and us on the other. Every time he made a move for us one way, we would lurch the other, which resulted in the three of us chasing in circles around and around the bus shelter.

Fortunately, what this brutish character had in strength and size, he could not match in dexterity. So Freddie and I made short work of avoiding his advances. I looked across to poor Mark, who had been thrown to the floor and was lying on his back, holding his face with one hand and trying to hold off his assailant with the other.

And then, as quickly as it had started, it finished. These brutes wanted nothing, no cash, no wallet, no passports; they simply wanted to pummel some tourists.

They make up for their miserable lives by making someone else feel more miserable. Cheap beer breeds brutes.

We sat on the side of the road, licking our wounds. Mark was by far the worse off, with his shirt ripped off his back and sizeable blows to the face, which were starting to bleed pretty heavily. I had taken a hefty blow to the side of the face. Fred, completely in character, emerged unscathed. And was pretty pleased about the fact.

We limped arm in arm back to the hostel and to Audrey, who, for the first time on the trip, would live up to her original purpose and bandaged us back together.

Bratislava won't live too fondly in the memory. But it served its purpose. It made us realise that we were no longer in Oxford. Having grown up in the South West of England, I think we expected everywhere to be as welcoming and friendly. The world is a small place now is an oft-quoted expression. But it's not that small. We were still in Europe, but the inequalities were stark. People still led tough lives and carried the matching resentment. If anything, the world becoming a smaller place puts these inequalities in a harsher contrast. Anyone can get a front-row seat to anyone else's life through social media and ponder the differences.

It's made me realise, looking back, now I'm at an age where I ask such questions, that your contentment and happiness aren't based on the quality of your life so much as they're based on the comparative quality of your life. We used to compare ourselves to those in our family, town, or village who, by definition, were on a similar footing. But now we compare ourselves to anyone with a phone and a camera. When you have a pool that big, there is always someone better off than you.

I'm thankful our battering happened when it did. If we had continued acting in that devil-may-care way as we headed further east, assuming everyone a friend and every day a party, the eventual battering might have been much worse. I felt guilty it was Mark who bore the brunt of the teachings; Freddie and I needed the lesson.

The next morning, I awoke fully clothed on top of the bed sheets with my shoes still on and toothbrush in hand. I shook the others awake and murmured something about coffee. We had to get going to meet our friend and trusted mechanic, Naoki. Mark was in a particularly wretched state. Freddie and I wrestled him out of his bed as he groaned and yelped as we grabbed hold of a sore rib or shoulder. We found two non-bruised bits to latch onto and dragged him to Audrey, where we opened up the back, let him fall onto one of the camp beds, and left him in the darkness.

If you draw your mind back to the car-park incident in Germany, one of Audrey's weaknesses was that she's a long-wheelbase vehicle — meaning there's a large gap between her front and back wheels — which means that ground clearance is a problem.

If the front and back wheels were on level ground, but between them was a bump, you were in trouble. It was incredibly easy to ground her and rip out her mechanical innards.

She also boasted air suspension, which, for the non-mechanically minded (a subset of the population that we were certainly part of) means that instead of having a spring to absorb shocks from the road, we had a glorified airbag beside each wheel which needed time to blow up before we departed each morning.

On that particular morning, we were in no mood to wait around and forgot to give Audrey's air suspension enough time to inflate. Which meant her already poor ground clearance was even worse.

You can probably guess what happened next. As I drove out of the carpark and over the apex of a small mound, there was an ear-piercing crunch and then what sounded like the dragging of a metallic object along the tarmac.

"OH, FOR FUCKS SAKE!" we screamed. This was the last thing we needed in our bruised and hungover state.

I nervously got out of the cab and got on all fours to assess the damage and found the whole exhaust and some other important-looking mechanical bits hanging off the underside of the van.

Why did this stuff always happen when *I* was driving? "Well, this is a shit state of affairs," I said to Freddie.

I knew our mechanical ability would be tested at some point — but I didn't think it would happen on four hours sleep, with a closed-over black eye, hungover and bruised from being beaten up the night before.

It's safe to say spirits were not high.

Mark had resigned himself to be incapable of helping — his eyes were so swollen he could barely see out of them. He crawled back into Audrey and went to sleep, leaving Freddie and I to contemplate how the hell we were going to get out of this mess. Driving to a mechanic wasn't an option as the undercarriage was dragging along the floor. We would have to patch her up here.

Freddie fetched the jack, and we lifted Audrey up so we could take a proper look underneath. We nervously crawled underneath the van, hoping that the jacks would hold.

Our main problem was that the exhaust pipe was massive. It was a good twelve feet from the engine at the front of the van to the exhaust at the back. And it was bloody heavy.

Fortunately, it had come off clean from its fitting with the engine. However, the binding was completely cracked, as were all the bindings anchoring the exhaust pipe to Audrey's underside.

Digging through all our supplies in the back of the van, being careful not to wake Mark, all we could find were plastic cable ties and wire. Freddie and I spent the next two hours securing the exhaust pipe back to the undercarriage using countless number of cable ties. We couldn't fix the exhaust pipe directly back onto the engine. The best we could do was "point" it in the right direction and hope it would catch the fumes. Did it matter that it wasn't tightly secured? We had no idea.

After two hours, we stood back to admire our work; it seemed okay. But we were terrified that the exhaust pipe would get hot, melt through the cable ties, and drop the whole lot onto the motorway when driving at speed, taking out the rest of the engine with it and causing a multi-car pileup.

This would continue to terrify us every time we breached 40mph for the rest of the trip. Luckily for us, that wasn't that often.

We suddenly remembered that we had to pick up our friend

Naoki from the train station. We had agreed to meet at 11 am, it was now 3 pm. And he was a mechanic! It suddenly felt as though the day was going to get much better, and we'd get to leave Slovakia without risking another pasting.

I slowly drove out of the car park with Freddie lifting up the exhaust so we wouldn't reground ourselves on the same mound, and gingerly crept along the road to the train station with all windows down, listening intently for any snapping of cable tie or crunch of metal on tarmac. We arrived in one piece, with Naoki patiently waiting for us.

I jumped out, greeted him like an old friend, and hurriedly explained what had happened. We looked underneath Audrey to find the exhaust pipe swinging back and forth — not ideal, but at least it wasn't on the floor.

Naoki thanked me for the detailed update but asked me with a hint of embarrassment exactly what I was expecting him to do.

"Well, you're a mechanic," I replied, "Fix it!" pointing back at the swinging exhaust pipe.

"Erm," he responded with now more than a hint of embar- rassment, "I work in Marketing."

I looked at him to see if he was going to crack into laughter. He didn't.

I searched my brain. At some point the night before, there must have been a disconnect between offering a lift to one person and someone completely different accepting.

"I did wonder why you were so keen to give me a ride," he would go on to say. "Enough of this city," I said, walking to the driver's seat.

Naoki jumped in the back, and I closed the door behind him. Strangely he didn't show any alarm at finding a comatose Mark in the back with him.

7

Romania

We set off for our longest drive yet — heading southeast crossing the border into Hungary, dropping Naoki off in Budapest and then on to Romania, driving the length of the country past Bucharest with our sights set on the coast of the Black Sea. From there, we would be in striking distance of Istanbul and Mark's departure.

As we drove, my mind reflected back to the night before. I tried to imagine the lives of our assailants. What would drive someone to beat up three complete strangers? I conjured up a picture of them working in a factory, performing menial tasks, being shouted at by suits and ties, and living for the weekend. A Saturday night beer their only release. No ambition nor prospects. Throwing their fists the only way to climb the ladder of self-esteem and gain notoriety. Regaling their friends and colleagues with the story of three howling Brits.

I had no idea if this was anywhere close to accurate. But it gave me some comfort that I could actually understand their motives.

If we had thought crossing the border into Slovakia rewound

the clock a decade or two, then crossing the border into Romania rewound it a century. The change was absolute, we stopped at the border to assess our options. Ahead, the road gave way from pristine tarmac to gravel, quite literally at the border. The rare parts of the road that were tarmacked were so covered in potholes and stray dogs it looked like a *Mario Kart* track. The road itself was straight as a die from here to the horizon, dissecting dense pine forests on either side. As if to complete the dramatic picture, the horizon was covered in dark foreboding clouds.

I looked at Freddie and shrugged. "I guess this is Romania." I put Audrey back into gear and slowly pushed her off the small ledge from tarmac to gravel and accelerated into our eighth country of the trip.

I'd always had a nagging interest to visit Romania ever since watching Dracula. Medieval castles perched upon rocky outcrops, steep grey-faced cliffs soaring over dense forests below and, of course, salivating vampires watching down from dark windows.

As we drove away from the border, we were quickly doused in dense forest, the light disappeared, and I couldn't shake the thought of the thugs from my mind. We pulled over to camp, too tired to even eat. I crawled through the little hatch between the cab and our quarters, not wanting to risk the outside. I found my bed and curled up.

We woke in the morning to the most spectacular scenery. Unbeknownst to us, we had parked in a lay-by at the edge of a cliff. I got out of the van, stretched, and looked out over the view ahead of us, all the stresses and worries from the night before washing away. The worries of the night always seem so ridiculous in the morning.

Standing on the edge of the cliff ahead of me was a valley of unbelievable lushness and beauty. Beneath my feet, I could see our road winding its way to the bottom, the slope so steep the road made its slow progress by turning back on itself at each corner. At the bottom of the valley laid a carpet of pine forest interspersed by small green meadows, darker than in England, surrounded by little villages with Alpine-style houses in miniature scale. And then further ahead, the valley rose once more up sheer grey cliff faces to yet more forest at the top. That side of the valley was in shade, the sun still low behind it, displaying the greenness of the valley floor in even greater contrast. Halfway down, I spotted an eagle soaring in the currents, around and around it went. Isn't it amazing seeing a bird flying from above?

I was feeling apprehensive but excited for what lay ahead. Europe had always felt like a warmup act to us. A chance to let off some steam before the action began. We always had Asia in the back of our minds, we knew that's when we would have to start to be a least a little more serious and prepared. But for the time being, whilst those worries were still ahead of us, we thought we might as well get stuck in and enjoy ourselves. But it was time to put the partying and drunkenness of Central Europe behind us; it was time to start the adventure.

I turned and headed back to Audrey, hands in pockets, head down, kicking the grass as I walked.

At each turn of our descent, we dropped into the valley, losing a little more of our bird's-eye view, the villages and fields growing larger and larger.

We took a road which dissected the country from west to east. The most direct route to Istanbul would have been straight south, but we wanted to see the Black Sea; for no other reason than it was there and why not. The road took us back up the other side of the valley, where we could look back across to our campsite. The road continued, following a winding mountain pass, with waterfalls gushing down onto the road, briefly pausing their descent, flowing over the road, before falling again. On we drove, tracing the course of a river through valleys and ravines, straining to see Dracula's lair around each corner.

As we reached the country's centre, the roads improved, coated in a lush tarmac that Audrey skipped over. We sailed past Bucharest. Screamed out of the windows at nothing in particular. This was the adventure I had come for.

But then the roads changed. Tarmac became gravel, which became potholed gravel, which became dirt. Audrey slowed to crawl, taking time to delicately tiptoe around potholes and other such hazards. Our confidence in making the coast fell. Her suspension was pushed to the limit, every crater that Audrey couldn't avoid would send us jumping from our seats, heads crashing into the ceiling and Audrey's exhaust pipe smacking into her undercarriage as it swung from side to side. But still, she continued, without a whimper of protest.

We had promised Mark the road from Bucharest to the Black Sea would only take six hours. It took 48. We camped *en route* and finally arrived late in the evening.

Christ, I thought, *if our route estimations were this wrong on the roads in Europe, what's going to happen when we hit the dust bowl of central Asia?* There wasn't a chance we're going to make it back in time for our jobs starting in September. So n*ot all bad*, I thought.

We had pinpointed Mamaia on the map, a coastal town on the Black Sea, expecting it to be a small fishing village, hoping to find a relaxed beach campsite and some good food. We arrived, however to find the Romanian version of Magaluf, full of drunk 16–25-year-olds trying to prove their wealth by slapping brands like Gucci and Prada across their chests and carrying the accompanying stern looks. I wasn't in the mood to indulge; we used Mamaia as a pit stop. We ate, slept, and moved on.

It's amazing how one event can change your mindset entirely. If we'd arrived in Mamaia just a week before, we would have set about the town with relish. The people I bemoan would likely have become good friends. But I had different eyes on now and could only see their materialism and unfriendly looks.

8

Bulgaria

Leaving Romania behind, we headed south towards Bulgaria, following a beautiful road that hugs the coast of the Black Sea towards the border. The road was good, and the sun was out. The stretch of coastline down through Bulgaria was as stunning as it was refreshingly deserted. Think the Amalfi without the Italians. Beach after beach and not a soul on them.

Crossing over the Bulgarian border was the first time we had to show our passports since leaving the UK — the beauty of Europe (Editor's Note: when I wrote this, that was not a politically charged comment!) Whilst we were fine to cross, the Bulgarian officials at the border — although very friendly — gave us considerable hassle as we didn't have Audrey's original ownership documents. We'd listened to someone back home who told us only to travel with photocopies in case we lost the originals. Don't listen to armchair travellers — lesson learnt.

After some negotiation, we managed to cross the border and swindled our way out of paying road tax by persuading the officials that we were driving a functioning emergency vehicle.

Happy with the day's mileage, we followed a very rutted track down to a beach, taking care to mount the ruts at slow speed to protect the exhaust pipe that continued to swing concerningly from side to side. At the end of the track was a perfect yellow sand beach, extending left and right as far as the eye could see and not a soul to interrupt the view. It was high tide, and the Black Sea lapped the shores gently as I cast out the line from our fishing rod and jammed the butt into the sand.

I sat back and watched the horizon as Freddie and Mark built up a fire that would, in all likelihood, have no fish cooked on it tonight. Wretched ration packs all round.

But just as I was losing faith, the end of the rod nodded, first timidly and then with huge force as it strained against its sandy berth.

"Fish!" I shouted as I leapt up to catch the rod as the sand gave way. "I think I might have actually caught a fish!"

"Come on, come on", I whispered to myself as I fought with the fish to bring it to shore. Twice the line got away from me as it whizzed back out to sea, following my unseen opponent.

Slowly it tired. With each wind of the reel, it came closer and closer to the beach until Freddie could wade out and grab the line above its mouth.

He raised it triumphantly above his head.

"We've got one!" we all cheered jubilantly, smiles etched across our faces.

I knocked its head on a stick and sat down. Smiling at Freddie and Mark in astonished silence.

I cleaned the fish and put a stick down its throat to suspend it over the fire. We stared into the fire as it gently cooked a delicious, soft, delicate texture with charred skin. Catching a fish on a deserted beach. Ok, now, this really was the adventure we had come for.

An electric storm started out to sea, sending crashing lighting and thundering rain down into the water. We watched on in silence as the storm rolled on south before falling into an utterly content sleep.

There's nothing quite like waking up on your own private beach and diving straight into the ocean. The revitalising water rushed up to meet me as I dived in headfirst. We cooked up some eggs for breakfast in the embers of the campfire and toyed with staying for a few days, trying to convince Mark to put off his damn job and stay with us.

"You've got all your life to work," I said as we all lay on our backs in the sand. "What could possibly be better than this?"

But our pleading fell on deaf ears. His ambition outstripped Freddie's and mine, *financial* ambition in any case. There was an intensity in his eyes that told me he was already back in London. His flight was in two days, and he'd be on it. He'd be living a different life, eating Pret sandwiches at a desk in Canary Wharf before the week was out.

We hauled ourselves up and dusted ourselves down. We'd be back, we all told ourselves, stealing one last look at the beach as I shook Audrey awake to take us to the Turkish border. I think she was also looking forward to a few days' rest.

We rattled back up the track, Audrey's wheels slipping and spinning and then gaining traction as she slowly awoke from her slumber. The exhaust pipe was always in my mind, mistaking the crack of a stick or clang of a rock as the death knell that would end our trip. If it happened at any fair speed, I was convinced it would take out the whole of her undercarriage, and that would be it; the naysayers would win, and we'd be on the flight with Mark.

The border crossing into Turkey took a lot longer as we had to organise visas and insurance, but the green card (road tax) was once again free due to our good friend Audrey the Ambulance. It was the first time we had crossed a border where no English was spoken, something that would become a theme for the rest of the trip and added another layer of complication.

Freddie's mum had given him a 1950's Turkish phrasebook, which was useless. "How much are these strawberries?" is not of much use when crossing a border. The crossing took a long, long time in the scorching heat of the Turkish midday sun.

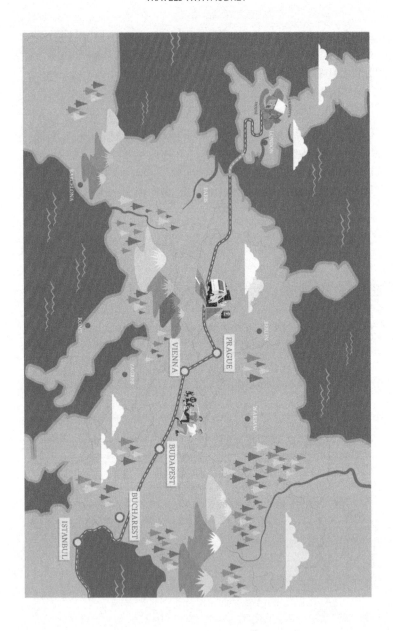

9

Instanbul

Your geography teacher will tell you that Istanbul is in Europe, well partly in any case. The Bosporus river that splits Istanbul in two is the border between Asia and Europe. Between East and West. But in reality, we'd already crossed over; Istanbul is an unmistakably Asian city.

Driving in, you first notice the minarets of mosques soaring into the air on every corner. Hundreds upon hundreds of them creating a stage for the muezzins to call worshippers to prayer. If you ever go to Istanbul, arrive in the late afternoon as the dying embers of the sun cast a golden haze over the entire city. The minarets turn into beacons of fire. I was in love with the city as soon as we arrived.

Everywhere there was noise and activity, the taxis hooting and their drivers shouting at you if you dared get in their way, muezzins wailing, "My friend, my friend!" called out as a street hawker puts his arm around you and quotes outrageous prices for unneeded goods, halving the asking price as you walked away. The young, vibrant and fiercely modern Instabulite lay around in shisha bars, blowing smoke out their nostrils as they laid the world to rights. The parties in Taksim Square, as Turkish music that only suits the tastes of the locals, flood the streets. Late-night street food vendors, hawking you one more kebab for the day: "Very good to soak the beer away," they'd convincingly attest. The booming horns of the cruise ships as you slipped an afternoon cocktail overlooking the Bosphorus. Everyone selling anything from cigarettes to ancient antiques. "Very good price for you, my friend."

This utterly romantic picture thankfully shook me out of my, in retrospect, shamefully predictable prejudice of the city. Anyone with a predilection for their own voice had told us how dangerous it would be. The clash of cultures, the threat of terrorism, yada-yada. It became clear that they'd only travelled to the city through the pages and sensationalised images of the Daily Mail, the enemy of empathy and understanding in this modern world.

In any case, if they had ever been to Istanbul, they'd know that the traffic will kill you far before any decent terrorist gets his chance. My God, the traffic. The screeching of tyres, blaring of horns and rush of adrenaline as yet another car careened across lanes or stopped dead in front of you for no apparent reason.

Again, the Stanford map let us down when we needed her most. The all-important road detail was skipped over in favour of some delicate contouring on a nearby mountain range. It goes without saying that we quickly got lost trying to find the tourist information point, which we had hoped would point us in the direction of a good hostel. Fortunately, the amiable locals, realising we were from out of town and lost, would pull over and point us in the right direction.

After many hours of being lost in the bustling traffic in the intense heat, we resorted to hailing a taxi, telling him where we were headed in broken English whilst plying his palm with a hand full of notes and then following him there. We considered offering Mark as a passenger to make sure he would stick to his task, but we feared we'd lose him to Istanbul forever.

The taxi driver set off at breakneck speed, with one arm on the steering wheel and the other pointing to an upcoming turn, with minimal notice, before he swerved across lines of traffic and down a side street. I had the unfortunate task of trying to keep up with this madman. Audrey has many assets, but dexterity isn't one of them. Like a whale trying to chase a fish through coral, we followed as the taxi nipped between cars and disappeared down alleyways without the slightest strain. The driver constantly flaying his arms to say, "Keep up!" as Audrey stumbled along behind, clipping off wing mirrors, corners of buildings and elderly relatives lagging behind their family. Before long, the taxi took one sharp turn too many, and we overshot. Slamming on the brakes, I looked in the wing mirrors as I reversed back. But when we got to the turning, the taxi had long gone, and so too our money, with us no closer to finding a bed for the night.

We eventually found a hostel within a short walk of the Blue Mosque, and we spent three glorious days eating and exploring our way around the ancient capital. Our much-maligned university diet of twice-daily kebabs was actively encouraged in this town. We dived in with relish.

The city has such incredible energy to it. As we walked its streets, vendors served up the most delicious fare at all hours of the day to packed tables and courtyards. Men sat around, slapping the backs of their neighbours as they delivered their punchline, leaning back and roaring with laughter into the night sky.

Istanbul heralded the end of our first chapter, not just the end of Europe but the end of Mark. He left us to pursue the riches of London, starting a job as an FX broker for reasons that he explained many times but are lost on me now.

At this point, our already shaky plan became a little shakier. If we were honest with ourselves, until now, we'd had an "if we actually reach Istanbul, we'll worry about it then" attitude, but that was of little help now that we'd actually made it.

Our loose plan was to head northeast, to hit the coast of the Black Sea and follow it along to the Iranian border and then to continue east towards the central Asian republics, through Uzbekistan.

But the day we were due to leave, I received an email from the Iranian embassy.

"After careful consideration, we have decided to deny you a visa to the Republic of Iran."

My heart sank; Iran was not only the country I was most looking forward to visiting, the exoticism of the place had really captured our imaginations, but it was also the keystone of our journey. Without Iran, there was no way east.

The email continued, "We are currently not accepting foreign vehicles into the country."

They hadn't rejected us; they had rejected Audrey. That stung particularly. Like having a child rejected from a school. *If only they knew her, like I knew her*, I thought.

Back to the drawing board. We sat in our hostel and spread our maps across our bed. After a great deal of finger tracing and strained concentration, we could see there were two options. We could either turn around and head north, back up through

Eastern Europe, back up through Bulgaria and Romania and then on to the Russian border and traverse pretty much the whole of Russia and Kazakhstan to hit Mongolia which would lead us to China. Or we could carry on through Turkey, head north through Georgia and into Russia that way. A much better plan, we thought. Largely down to my male ego, I can't bear to retrace my steps and drive back down an already-trodden road when you can explore somewhere new.

We set about getting the necessary visas for our new route. Georgia was easy, Russia was a different story. Further research revealed that the border between Russia and Georgia had been closed since the war between the two countries two years before. I chastised myself for not knowing more about the world as our frustration mounted. There's nothing like travelling to remind you how little you know and how naive you are of events outside of your tiny corner of the world.

Back, again, to the drawing board. Our key issue was the biblical-sounding Caspian Sea that is wedged between east and west. Russia to its north, Kazakhstan and Turkmenistan to its East, Iran to its south and the Caucasus to its west. It was like a big middle finger protruding from the map. Stopping all those with adventure in mind and fuel in their tank from venturing any further.

From where we were in Turkey, the only border open to us was Georgia. Once we were in Georgia, the only open border was to cross into Azerbaijan, but from there, all that was ahead was the coast of the Caspian. No roads east.

After a long afternoon prodding a keyboard in an internet cafe, we found a *Lonely Planet* forum that mentioned a cargo ship that left Baku in Azerbaijan and crossed the Caspian Sea bound for the secretive dictatorship of Turkmenistan, which would put us back on route. It felt high-risk, putting our hopes on the report from some guy in an internet forum. But it was our only option. Baku it was to be.

As had become already typical, we got horribly lost leaving Istanbul. Freddie confidently navigated us onto an incredibly narrow and steep cobbled street, claiming it was the principal exit thoroughfare of Istanbul. Its cobbles so slippery and shiny you could quite comfortably shave in their reflection. The incline ahead was less a major motorised thoroughfare leading out of the city but an escarpment for mountain goats. This would be a problem for the lightest and most dexterous hatchbacks. But for Audrey, who has a considerable weight issue — *I whisper quietly*— this is a brow mopping anxiety-riddled dilemma of the first order. She weighs in at a wheel slipping, gravity inducing and hand break straining 3,500 kgs. Which was only exacerbated by the four full reserve fuel tanks we had just filled up for our journey across Turkey.

"Are you sure this is the right way, mate?" I asked Fred, hoping we'd taken another wrong turn. But Freddie, like most men, has an inability to reverse out of an already voiced opinion.

"One hundred per cent, mate. This leads straight onto the motorway," Freddie replied, pointing at the map.

I looked back up the narrow cobbled street in disbelief that this would form a motorway slipway.

With some muttered words of encouragement to Audrey, I edged her slowly forward and then floored the accelerator, trying to build up speed on the run-up with the confidence of a debutant pole vaulter without the luxury of a crash mat. She hit the initial incline, and we were pressed back into our seats as she groaned up the face of the monstrous slope. She made commendable distance, initially. A thought that I hope was shared with the crowd of pedestrians stopping to watch the show.

But then her wheels started spinning, screeching against the tarmac as they did so before regaining traction, but then slipping again. The loss of traction came at ever-shortening intervals until her wheels just spun and screamed wildly as smoke streamed in from the windows.

Initially, we remained in the same spot with the soundtrack of Audrey groaning from under my feet and her wheels screaming for help. But then the poor old girl began to give in and started to slip backwards down the hill. Slowly, to begin with, before picking up momentum.

I began to panic, my foot pressing the accelerator to the floor, my knees straining, yet still, we slipped backwards. A feeling of complete helplessness washed over me.

I considered jumping out the door and letting fate deal with her and Freddie.

Hands dripping with sweat, I slammed two feet on the brake and pulled up the handbrake. She stopped, thank God. I slowly took my foot off the brake, and Audrey lurched backwards again. Foot straight back on the brake.

What now? I attempted to restart our ascent, but every time I took my foot off the brake, she'd lurched back even further.

I looked behind; a traffic jam of angry Istanbulites was forming and refusing to reverse. We had about 2 metres before we would touch the bumper of the leader.

"Let me take over," Freddie offered, clearly in the belief that this was all down to my inept driving.

Normally I would react with my ego. Particularly with

Freddie. But on this occasion, I was just relieved.

Swapping sides, I stayed in my seat with my foot on the brake until Freddie could replace his foot with mine as he jockeyed over the handbrake from his seat to mine. I made sure to walk around the front of Audrey to avoid the angry glares of the restless mob behind.

I examined her tires. As I thought, bald as a baby. "Idiot," I muttered to myself. I knew we should have changed them in Bulgaria.

In a rare moment of planning ahead, we had packed some old carpet to help if we ever got bogged down in mud. But they might just work here to add some friction between the wheels and the road. I got out and placed the carpet behind each back wheel.

I motioned to Fred, and he released the brake and reversed back over the carpet. On my command, he floored it.

"Now!"

For a brief moment, the carpet held, and Audrey crept forward. But then, in the blink of an eye, both pieces of carpet shot out at the speed of light and smashed into the windshield of the car behind.

The gentleman driving, who had given up watching our sorry attempts, jumped out of his seat with fright as the carpet smacked against his windshield. The plastic underside hit first and made a smack like a gunshot which caused the driver quite some alarm.

He leapt out of his car, screaming at us and gesticulating wildly. I had no idea what he was saying, but "you stupid fucking foreigners!" probably wasn't far off.

Being the man that I am, instead of trying to calm the situation, I ran back to the passenger seat, forgetting that our prized carpet was still stuck to his windshield.

"Well, I'm not fucking getting them; this was your idea," Freddie said helpfully. "This was your fucking route!" I offered in reply.

I caved and climbed back out of the van. Our friend in the car behind watched in disbelief as I then walked around and peeled the two pieces of carpet off his windshield before returning to Audrey. All without looking at him once.

"Right, let's give this one more go. If it doesn't work, we're just going to have to reverse down the hill," Freddie said.

"Well, you can try and explain that to our new friend in the car behind," I replied.

Then, with the most amount of concentration I had ever seen Freddie give to anything (and we sat next to each other during our university final exams), he managed to find the right level of slow revs that persuaded Audrey to edge ever so slowly up the hill. We crept up inch by inch until we reached the top, where we pulled over, incredibly relieved, to let the traffic through. People congratulated us on our endeavours by gesticulating and shouting every swear word under the sun in Turkish first, and then English just to make sure we got the point. We counted twenty cars in our self-made traffic jam — not bad for a morning's work.

Now we were over the other side of the hill; I looked for Freddie's promised slipway onto the motorway. Was it there? Of course, it fucking wasn't. We turned around and drove back down that bastard of a hill.

On the second attempt, we found the motorway that led us east out of Istanbul. As we left, we crossed over the Bosporus river, a wonderfully turquoise torrent of water that splits Turkey in two, thronged with sailing boats and cruise ships and lined by glitzy bars and mosques, which was a perfect metaphor as crossing the straight signalled our departure from Europe and our arrival into Asia: the second continent that we planned to span in its entirety.

We had made it through Europe. My biggest fear of not making it out of our home continent hadn't come to fruition. We had made it with just a cracked roof, broken exhaust pipe and facial bruising to show for our troubles. But the most invigorating thing was that we were getting better each and every day, bouncing from each near disaster to the next, but learning from them and, in doing so, leaving our inexperiences behind.

We now let the suspension inflate fully before leaving each morning, we never let Mark make size judgements and most importantly, we will never, ever, let Freddie map read. It put us on such a high, like a surfer riding a big wave as we crossed that bridge. Our naivety and inexperience that was illustrated in harsh light in Europe, flowing away into the Bosporus. We were now better placed to face the undoubted challenges Asia would throw at us.

We estimated it would take us four days to cross the rest of Turkey, our route would take us along the Pontic Mountain range, the spine of the country from west to east. And then down onto the coast of the Black Sea, which we would follow till Georgia.

We wound our way up into the Pontics, getting higher with each turn and as we did so, the heat, thankfully, reduced. In the distance were always mountains, over the whole scene hung an amazing light that you don't get in other parts of the world, like someone has placed a filter over the sun, casting a glaze of gold and lilac over the landscape. Every contour, tree, bush and passing goat stands out in vivid sharpness.

That night we camped just outside a small mountain village and played football in the valley before cooking up a chicken bought from a local market over the fire. Our camp beds were set up on high ground, perfectly placed for sunrise, where we fell asleep.

The following morning, we woke to the most spectacular view of a golden sunrise cast across the mountain range beneath us.

We took a very leisurely breakfast cooking eggs on the embers of the fire, and then set about our now strictly enforced (after the debacles of Frankfurt, Prague, and Istanbul) morning inspection of Audrey, checking her tyres, oil, and suspension. Walking around her like a sergeant major inspecting his platoon, kicking things and prodding others. We even went to the lengths of taping a piece of paper onto the dashboard, which read, "Remember the fucking suspension!" to remind ourselves each morning. See, we were learning.

We crossed the remainder of the mountain range and arrived on the Black Sea coast just after lunchtime. After turning our nose up at a number of beaches, we eventually found a place to camp beside a Turkish tea shop with a resplendent coastal view. Tea is something the Turkish people drink in remarkable quantities. We made good friends with the tea shop workers who were of a similar age, and even though we had no common language, we chatted for ages by randomly naming English and Turkish footballers. Football is quite the global language. Unfortunately, they were Chelsea fans.

"Beckham," one would shout.

"Yes, very good!" we would reply "Gerrard!" "Good!

Rooney!"

"No! Not good!"

And so the conversation would go on for quite some time. Despite our lack of a common language, we got on wildly.

We had begun a tradition of inviting everyone we had met to sign their name and to leave a message on the back of Audrey. It started with friends and family wishing us good luck. The artwork was now filling up nicely and starting to spread down the sides like a tattooed sleeve.

"Chelsi, Good!" Wrote one of them. The other, taking inspiration from his mate, went one better with "Chelsi, very good!"

After the heat and stresses of Istanbul, spending the afternoon in the Black Sea was the rejuvenation we needed. We lay in the sea, letting the muck, sweat and stresses wash off our bodies. I often ask myself what I like most, the energy and excitement of the city, or the peace and relaxation of the countryside. But I've come to realise they only work in contrast to each other. That night we kept ourselves busy playing cricket on the beach, roping in some bemused locals to sit in the slips (we had managed to leave behind Audrey's ownership documents, but two cricket bats and many balls had made it) before falling into a contented sleep in the back of the van.

The following morning, we woke early, washed in the sea, and continued our slow trudge along the coast to Georgia. Repeating the same formula each day, driving till lunch, finding a good restaurant on the beach and then spending the afternoon messing about on small deserted beaches under the warm of the Turkish sun — we took this part of the journey slow, our only job for each day just getting that little further east. We were in no hurry and it was glorious.

10

Georgia

After several days we made it to the Georgian border, where we faced the same problem as the previous border crossing. No original ownership documents for Audrey. We showed them our photocopies and explained that the originals were waiting for us at the Post Office in Tbilisi (where my parents had sent them) but no matter. Although they were very friendly, took great interest in Audrey, wrote welcome messages, and drew pictures on her back, they wouldn't let us through the border.

The border guards called over the boss, who zoomed in on a Segway, of all things. It was a surreal sight; most of the officers didn't have uniforms, but the boss had a Segway. And he was very proud of his toy and obvious status symbol and would make a great show of whizzing from person to person when a step or two, or indeed a slightly raised voice, would have sufficed.

Once fully briefed on our situation, he thought for a moment and then repeated the party line: "No original, no entry," and would continuously repeat this every time we tried to interject in a robotic manner that gave off the sure impression that there was to be no reasoning with this man.

"No original, no entry." "But it's..."

"No original, no entry."

"Yes, I understand that, but..." "No original, no entry."

"Yes, I'm with you, but..." "NO ORIGINAL, NO ENTRY."

We gave up.

As I have stressed already, if we were denied entry into Georgia, it would break our dream of driving through central Asia, we would instead have to turn around and circumnavigate three of the four sides of the Black Sea by driving all the way back through Turkey up through Eastern Europe and then across the length of Russia just to get back on track. It would mean many thousands of miles added to our journey, not to mention a much less interesting route.

Understandably, we were feeling slightly forlorn and, in the hot, arid border area, starting to get frustrated. Somehow every border we crossed seemed to be about ten degrees hotter than the surrounding countryside.

Suddenly, he spotted the Liverpool scarf on the front seat, and his eyes lit up. "Ahh, Liverpool very good, yes?"

"Liverpool. Me. Yes," I responded, pointing at myself and speaking in that embarrassing pidgin that the English adopt when speaking with people in foreign lands. "Yes, yes — Liverpool!" frantically trying to find some common ground with the man.

Freddie, trying to jump on the bandwagon, then held aloft his QPR scarf (a particularly poor football team from West London that Freddie has the misfortune of supporting), but this was met by a very confused look on the boss man's face. Freddie quickly put the scarf away, realising it was only hindering the process. This new-found common ground seemed to grease the wheels of our crossing, and after a bit more deliberating, they agreed to let us pass through as long as when we exited Georgia, we could produce the original ownership documents. We promised on all our lives that we would and thanked them profusely.

"The only time you've ever benefited from being a Liverpool fan," Freddie smirked as we drove away after a mere six hours spent crossing the border. It was getting dark as we drove our first miles into Georgia and quickly found a camp spot just outside the seaside town of Batumi.

As we'd had a pretty restful week along the Turkish coast, Freddie and I decided it was high time for a night out. We hitched a ride into Batumi to check out the local action. Amazingly, at the restaurant we picked, the couple at the next-door table were British working for the Red Cross out here. Recognising our accents, they quickly asked how we had come to be in Batumi.

"Oh, we drove."

"What do you mean you drove? From where?" Shock showed clearly on their faces.

"From Oxford!" This conversation became fairly standard for us and would be met by more and more of a surprised reaction and then of suspicion the further we got from home.

Intrigued by this, they invited us on a tour of Batumi's best bars, which ended up in the early hours in a club on the waterfront where groups of men were dancing in squat position, kicking their knees out to the music. It was a move that required muscles in places that had long since disappeared for Freddie and me. A fact that delighted the locals as we ended up on our arses time after time.

Waking up in the back of Audrey is horrific, even if you haven't got a hangover. It was approaching midsummer in the Caucasus, and each morning we'd be woken up, coated in sweat as we drew in our first gulp of stale hot air for the day. The first-up would madly wrestle off his sleeping bag and then dive over to swing open the slide doors and drink in the gloriously cool and crisp air.

The aim that day was to reach the capital of Tbilisi on the eastern side of Georgia by driving through the heart of the country. It would be a journey that kick-started our love affair with the countryside of this spectacular place.

After the harsh and arid terrain of eastern Turkey, Georgia was a green and wonderful land. We drove by lush fields intersected by gushing gorges running down from the mountaintops of its intensely politicised border with Russia in the north.

In the rare moments that I was bored of staring at the landscape, I read about Georgia and its rich history littered with invasions. Perhaps unsurprising considering it's sandwiched between the two warmongering nations of Turkey and Russia. Not to mention the Azerbaijanis to the east who aren't scared of a scuffle either.

The land has been brutally claimed by everyone from Alexander the Great to Genghis Khan. The Romans, Mongols, Ottomans, Persians and Russians have each tried to wipe the slate clean and impose their own culture. And each, I'm happy to report, failed.

Despite all of this, despite the constant international interference and long periods of occupation. Georgia has been able to maintain a culture that is unmistakably Georgian. Take, for example, their alphabet, which is completely unique. If you are as uncultured as I am, when you see Georgian letters, you'll immediately think of the Elvish writing in Lord of the Rings. Full of elegant swishes and rounded syllables with dots above. Charming, but causes issues when map reading.

The Georgians also have their own religion, both official and unofficial. The latter being rugby, which is a national obsession. I'd be surprised if there is a rugby pitch within 3,000 miles in either direction of the Georgian border, but inside their border, they occupied the common ground in every town and village we drove through. And their stars, big brutes of men, adorned every banner and advertising promotion we passed. I would love to know how their obsession with this sport started and grew.

About two hours out of Tbilisi, we drove through the town of Stalin's birth, Gori, which acts as the perfect metaphor for and barometer of the political ventings of Georgians. Some, particularly the older generations, remember Stalin as the man who defeated Hitler. Others remember him as the dictator who condemned millions to their deaths. And your view on Stalin likely dictates your view on whether Georgia should lean east or west. And thus, statues of Stalin are either pulled down or built back up, depending on who's ruling this nation, in a show of populist nonsense we've come to call progress in the modern political age.

Many Georgians are scared of Russia, and with due reason, much of what was Georgia is now Russia. And they feel they should cosy up with Europe and the US. To such an extent, Georgians fought alongside the Americans in Afghanistan and are seriously considering joining the EU. Much to the chagrin of Putin. But others, again the older population, are nostalgic for the Soviet Union and the guaranteed housing and employment it provided.

And it was with those eyes that we arrived in Tbilisi, the capital of Georgia. Everything seemed to be either European possibility or Soviet remembrance. In our eyes, the cities' architecture, once the veil was lifted, showed glimpses of Prague or Budapest. But with very vivid Soviet scars across its face in the form of brutalist apartment buildings. But of course, to others, the picture would be completely the opposite.

The old town, with the rushing Kura river flowing through its centre, is crumbling. It feels as if every third building has cracks running through some very important-looking part of its structure, with vines and flowers creeping through where bricks ought to be. Which both gave it its charm and also taught you to be very selective over where you choose to stay.

The town runs up a hill towards the Narikala fortress, an amazing medieval castle which stands guard overlooking the city below. The views from the top give a panoramic view of the city, and the hundreds of terracotta red roofs with the blue Kura river snaking through, carrying crisp meltwater from the mountains you can see in the distance. The park on the furthest bank holds the daily markets where you could buy fascinating old Soviet relics, military uniforms, guns, and medals of honour from battles past.

We found a hostel in the old town and some much-needed new company; adventurous European gap year students mostly, who we assembled for a night out. The Georgians were very passionate about wine, which came as a surprise to Freddie and me. They make a lot of it (and it's good!) and drink even more. The evening was spent tasting our way through many a bottle and pausing, seemingly every thirty seconds, to toast some God, Georgian poet, favourite mountain, or Georgia itself and then downing our glasses after each toast alternating between a local bottle of seriously good wine and a spirit called Chacha — with someone on a nearby table having a seemingly endless supply. By the end of the night, it actually tasted okay.

Every Georgian we met was obsessed with The Beatles, and every bar we walked into bellowed out their greatest hits on repeat. Each night would end with a group of us sweating, jumping around, arm in arm, belting out *Hey Jude*.

Tbilisi had the feeling of a frontier town, the last stop for refuge before tackling a large and impressive mountain. I always find I get along in these places, extreme places with extreme people. No half measures. Scaling a mountain one weekend, partying to 6 am the next. No in-betweens.

It's strange thinking back; as you cross from West to East, you alternate from teetotaling Arabic countries to countries in which you were encouraged to drink your body weight each evening. The warmongering nature of this part of the world seems to have pushed opposing cultures further and further into the extremes.

Due to our sudden change of route after being refused entry into Iran, we didn't have our visas for Azerbaijan, our next destination. We took our passports to the embassy but were told it would take three days to process. We were also waiting on Audrey's ownership documents which were due to turn up at the Tbilisi post office in a matter of days.

So we decided to get out and explore more of the country. We were itching to go and check out the border with Russia to see if it was as highly charged (and beautiful) as everyone had been telling us. It's hard to have a conversation with a Georgian without Kazbegi, the border outpost, coming up either because of its beauty or because of the "damned Russians".

The road to Kazbegi scaled the Greater Caucasus Mountains over the infamous Jvari Pass. Stalin tried to build a tarmac road over the pass when Georgia was under Soviet rule but was defeated by the elements. The poor sods who lived on the other side of the pass were cut off from civilisation for six months a year when the snow came. It sounded ripe for an adventure.

As we started to drive across the plains north of Tbilisi, the mountains rose up ahead of us towards the Russian border. The road headed straight as a die towards the base of the mountains. Completely flat plains surrounded the road on all sides for about fifty miles until they reached the base of the mountain and rose vertically to the sky. No foothills or any suggestion of what lay ahead. The plane just intersected straight onto the first rising shoulder of the mountain. I've never been anywhere quite like it.

We pulled into a petrol station to fill up and ask about conditions ahead. There were a group of young men killing time, sitting around on their haunches smoking, as there always seem to be in this part of the world. They were wearing several generations-old tweed jackets, had weather-beaten faces with long protruding noses and were sucking on rolled cigarettes that needed relighting after each drag. One of them was far younger than the others, and he jumped up as we arrived and introduced himself warmly.

"Hello, my name Alexi" as he grabbed my hand with both of his and shook hard. "Hi, I'm Max; this is Freddie."

"Where you from?" he asked with excitement in his eyes. "England."

"England, is it!" he inhaled as his eyes grew wider, and he turned to his friends to make sure they were listening in. "Wow, you drive this?" he walked over to Audrey and traced his hand over her body. "Where you go now?" turning back to us.

"To Kazbegi," I said, pointing over the mountains.

"Kazbegi! No, not possible in this," he said, pointing at Audrey and then wagging his finger. He turned to his friends, who had grown bored and turned in amongst themselves. He shouted something in Georgian, which must have been pretty funny as they all rolled back and laughed into the skies holding their bellies. The most senior of the group got up and strolled over to us, and the others followed at a distance. A serious conversation followed between Alexi and his senior. After a pause for reflection, he turned back to us and shook his head solemnly.

"I'm sorry, in this, not possible Kazbegi," he said as if he was a border guard with power to deny us entry. I turned to Freddie to gauge his reaction. He shrugged. Alexi could see he wasn't getting through.

"It..." he paused, frustrated he couldn't remember the right English word and said something in Georgian that I'm guessing meant, "It's very steep," as he motioned with his hand at a sharp angle. He then made some noises with his mouth that could have either been rushing water or growling wolves. He looked at us with a concerned face to make sure his argument landed.

After pausing for dramatic effect, he said, "But, I take you." It wasn't posed as a question. "500 Lari."

I turned to Freddie. "What do you think, mate?"

"They're just trying to make some money. Let's give it a shot, if it gets too steep, we'll turn back," Freddie replied.

"But, what about the wolves?" I replied.

Fred looked at me, confused; he clearly hadn't interpreted

the noises the same way. I turned back to Alexi. "No, thank you, Alexi. We will try."

He stared at me intensely as if to gauge my sanity and then flicked his hand in the air in a resigned fashion as he turned back to his friends and went back to sucking on cigarette butts.

We turned out of the petrol station and headed onwards. The anxiety generated by Alexi and his friends was calmed by the spectacular landscape, which got bigger and bigger with each mile we drove. Rock faces screamed up into the air as waterfalls crashed down around them, scree falls creating chicanes in the road.

After about an hour of driving, we reached the start of the mountain pass. The ascent started smoothly, winding its way around the side of the mountain. Halfway up, the tarmac ran out, and we dropped onto a single-laned coarse gravel track, weathered and beaten by the elements. Enormous potholes required considerable concentration to avoid whilst Freddie leaned out of the window to assess our distance from the edge. "You've got about a meter! Okay, now half a meter. A quarter of a meter! Okay, stop, stop. Stop. Max! Max! Stop!" each bellow getting louder and more anxious.

The weather, mercifully, was set fine, with just a few clouds capping the peaks above. Affording us a clear view back down the valley for the rare moments when we took our eyes off the road.

This narrow gravel track clung to the hillside at a right angle as we wound our ascent up the mountain. Shrines dotted the road remembering the lives of the road's victims lay at unnervingly regular intervals.

Every now and again, we would be forced to the side of the road as trucks carrying Georgian troops heading to or returning from the Russian border would delicately work their way around us.

"After you, boys" we would cry, more than happy for someone to show us the way, relieved to see another heavy vehicle on the road.

When these big trucks were travelling in the opposite direction, we would have to reverse back down the road to a crossing point. Each of which would be up to a mile apart. When presented with a showdown of who would reverse back to the nearest crossing point, a truckload of armed Georgian soldiers or two scrawny British guys, we would always blink first. And they knew that as well as we did.

This reversing ordeal would involve Freddie jumping out and slowly guiding Audrey back, ever so slowly, down the hill. With no rearview mirror, I had to rely on my wing mirrors and Freddie, who would often be pointing two different ways simultaneously. One such manoeuvre took thirty minutes of reversing before we found the crossing point. The soldiers cheered as they eventually passed us by. Their faces a mixture of smiles and complete confusion as to what a British ambulance was doing halfway up one of the most dangerous mountain passes in Georgia on the way to one of the world's most active political fault lines.

They never stopped to ask. Probably exhausted by months on the front line and desperate to get back to their families.

At times, we did question the ridiculousness of the situation we found ourselves in. This wasn't even on our route. The only reason we were driving this road was because we had time to kill, and what better way to kill time than visit Kazbegi, an active military zone?

It's difficult to describe the sense of fear the ravines struck in us as we tried to keep all four wheels on the road. They wouldn't so much drop-down, but drop-in. If you stopped and got out to look over the edge, which I would strongly advise against, you wouldn't be able to see the first twenty metres of the drop because it would go directly inwards and underneath you, forcing the road into an unnerving overhang over the precipice and raging torrent below. You would not only have to pay particular attention to not go over the edge but also to not go anywhere near the edge, as you had no idea how strong the overhang would be. There was no definite edge to follow. And with Audrey, the four-tonne beast that she is, we were taking no chances.

As we got higher and higher, winding our way around shoulder after shoulder of the pass, the clouds that were previously just a pretty backdrop — a contrast to the surrounding blue skies — now started to engulf us. Rendering visibility down to a few tens of meters. Making the already difficult job of keeping Audrey on the straight and narrow practically impossible. It then started to rain. Hard.

With channels of water quickly appearing on the road and the words of one of the locals telling us that landslides were common in the rain ringing in our ears, we decided to park up and wait it out.

We passed time by playing cards in the front, praying that no mad Georgians would come careering around the corner as, in this visibility, we would get about a ten-second warning before they hit us.

After an hour or two, the rain passed, and we set off again. But now on ground that was not just unstable, but wet and slippery too. Our top speed over the entire ascent was around 7mph, and gears three, four and five became complete strangers.

Whoever was driving was locked into a forward-leaning position over the steering wheel, eyes narrowed, arms tight. We laughed to ourselves that the friendly Georgians who offered their cars probably had more of our safety in mind than we gave them credit for.

However, despite all of this, Audrey, with her new tires, coped remarkably well. Apart from a few wheel spins and slips on the steeper parts of the road and wet rocks, she glided up that mountain pass.

The key thing to remember with Audrey, as we discovered the hard way in Eastern Europe, was that she had a very low ground clearance. Any slip of a wheel from higher ground to lower ground could rip out her entire undercarriage. However, if you were mindful of that and chose a path that meant the undercarriage was raised high and you never dropped one set of wheels from high terrain to low without doing the opposite with the other set of wheels, she was okay. Most of the time.

Her traction on the steep and slippery ground was remarkable. We were very proud. Patting her on the dashboard as she traversed each challenge. Finally, after a few false dawns, we reached the summit. We got out and posed for pictures next to a mound of rocks that signified the spot. The clouds, very briefly, parted to reveal how far and how high we had come.

It was the middle of July by this point, but my God, it was cold. We were wearing all the cold weather gear we had, but we hadn't really packed for this sort of climate.

The relief, once we came down the other side onto a spectacular plain with the mountains rising up behind, was absolute. Like diving into a pool on a hot summer's day. The relief washes over you. The muscles in my shoulders and back that had spent the last two hours in a state close to rigour mortis, started to relax, and my shoulders dropped.

The landscape was unbelievably beautiful; it felt like we were in Switzerland in spring. Bright green fields with impossibly blue lakes mirror the snow-capped mountains ahead.

As we approached the village of Kazbegi, sheepdogs rushed out to greet us, yapping at our tyres. We were later told that they were trained to guard against the many wolves in the area and were notoriously ferocious. It was the wolves Alexei was warning us about, after all. We had three days to kill in this alpine wonderland.

Kazbegi is renowned for its spectacular churches, pitched at the top of huge mountains and on the edges of cliffs that make you gaze in wonder as to how they lugged everything up there. The area is incredibly religious and rich in history and myth. It's hard not to allow your imagination to run wild as you shelter around a fire with yet more local Chacha and a strong gale outside whipping around the mountain tops as you're regaled with tales of the past.

On one such evening, we were told how, according to the Greeks, as punishment for teaching mankind how to make fire, the Titan Prometheus was chained to a mountainside in the Caucasus for all eternity. The Georgians believe it was the icy slopes of Kazbegi, the main mountain upon which the Kazbegi village was set, to which he was chained. Prometheus was supposedly imprisoned in a cave 4,000 meters high. The cave, now called Betlemi (Bethlehem), later served as a dwelling for orthodox monks and was said to have contained many sacred relics, including Abraham's tent and Christ's manger. I was all for such tales, as they brought life and mystery to our surroundings.

Mt. Kazbegi itself is a serious climb: three or four days with proper equipment needed and only a 50% success rate. So instead, we spent our time trekking around its foothills.

A wonderfully entrepreneurial local made his living by sprinting thrill-seeking hikers up to the first ridge in his Lada, a popular car in these parts. Instead of trekking up the steep, tree-enclosed first ridge, for a small fee, he would drive you up it. From where he picked us up the track certainly didn't look like a surface suitable for cars, barely even for hikers, but it was a long way away, and we gave him the benefit of the doubt.

Now, if you're ever in Kazbegi don't make the mistake we made of paying too much attention to the extraordinary number of dents in the side of his car, it puts you in a poor frame of mind for the ascent. One such dent would be better described as a crater and rendered the passenger door unusable.

He introduced himself as "Mr Schumacher", which I thought was an ironic joke given the age of his car. But as we reached the first bend, I realised he actually believed it, firmly. His foot pressed to the floor, his hand cycling through the gears at speed and a steely determination on his face. "Today, I go for record," he said as he looked across at me, smiling, trying to gauge my reaction, taking his eyes off the road for a concerning length of time.

Freddie and I grappled over our shoulders for non-existent seat belts. We resorted to pushing ourselves back into our seats with our hands pressed against the seats in front, wailing Hail Marys, as he accelerated into the first corner.

He didn't so much drive up that first ridge as bounce up it. My spine compressed into my pelvis as he lurched from pothole to pothole, keeping his arms straight and hands gripped to the steering wheel as he pushed his poor Lada into yet another boulder.

Clearly not content with the level of danger he had already bestowed upon us, he started to entertain us with some visual jokes such as pretending to fall asleep at the steering wheel, the brakes not working just as we approached a corner, and harmless jokes of that nature. He was clearly having the time of his life, slapping me on the knee after each gag. Freddie and I, meanwhile, had started holding hands two corners back.

As we arrived at the summit, I'm quite sure clearing air off the final incline, I sat back in my seat, shut my eyes, and exhaled deeply. But Mr Schumacher made it clear that time was money and waved us out of the car and motioned in the next batch of death wishers who were waiting at the top. They looked at us with concern as Freddie fell out of the car, stumbled two steps and then collapsed onto the floor, groaning. Mr Schumacher, however, was a man of efficiency and little sympathy. He extracted his fee off of Freddie as he was still on the floor and shepherded in the next batch. Like lambs to the slaughter.

The next few days were wonderful; with Audrey parked up in a church car park, we would wake up and gaze skyward, pick a peak and then spend the day climbing it whilst being careful to avoid the entrepreneurial advances of Mr Schumacher. Return-ing in the late afternoon to a thoroughly warming Georgian meal of either dumplings (which looked, but fortunately didn't taste, like oversized testicles), soup or kebabs. On our second to last day, we decided to push it a little further. Our last unclaimed peak soared beyond the others and was an overnight hike, according to the locals.

The day was sharp, but the skies were blue, and sunlight bounded around. Crystal clear visibility to the horizon. If we were going to do it, this was the day for it. We diligently packed up our rucksacks with rations and overnight necessities. And fashioned a tent out of an old gazebo by taking off its legs so that its roof provided some waterproofing.

We made the summit in the late afternoon and enjoyed the best views yet; sweeping all around us, we could see the Jvari pass we had driven over to our right and to our left, the Russian border. We strained our eyes to see if we could see any 'damned Russians.' Behind us, Mt Kazbegi still soared into the heavens above.

We began our descent and found a beautiful place to camp just as it was getting dark. It left us about a half-day hike the following morning to return to Audrey. We started the business of making camp.

Every campfire is awash with stories of hikers finding themselves plunged into mists and swirling rains when just shortly before, all before them was blue and clear. These stories were cliches, but, like most cliches, they are often true.

First, the sunshine vanished, and the temperature plummeted, like walking into the cold storeroom in a bottle shop. The winds picked up, threatening to lift the gazebo off its grounding, and brought with them mist and then rain.

I looked around, spotted a ridge that would provide cover, and shouted over to Freddie. We picked up our belongings and hauled them, heads down into the wind, to our new campsite, which brought relief from the gails at least.

I was wet with sweat and starting to worry as we dived under the tent. Actually, let's call it what it is, the roof of a god-damn gazebo. Designed for summer soirees and regattas, not extreme weather at 3,000 feet.

Freddie was not seeing the seriousness of our situation yet.

"I'm pretty chuffed with this," said Freddie laying claim to the gazebo idea with a contented look on his face as the waterproofing held. We had debated the merits of sleeping under a gazebo on the side of a mountain at 3,000 feet, but the draw of that one last unclaimed peak was just too strong.

I watched as the raindrops tapped on the thin waterproof sheeting above my head, increasing in their intensity. *This isn't going to hold*, I thought to myself.

Fred was busying himself thinking about his dinner, pulling out the necessary equipment.

For dinner was two of our prized but foul-tasting army ration packs. Although light, the required heating equipment was certainly not, as the bruising on my back from where the hex burner cut in would testify.

"Max, where are the pots to boil the ration packs in?" Freddie asked. "What are you talking about? They're in your bag," I replied.

"No, they are not," said Freddie, showing me the empty contents of his bag. "Don't tell me we left them behind?"

"Well, can you see them anywhere?" "But that means we can't cook our food!" "Yes. Welcome to the party, Einstein!"

And then I remembered, I had taken them out of the bag to let them dry in the sun after breakfast.

I crashed onto my back, hands holding my head. Missing a meal was a disaster on any day but on a day you've spent all your energy scaling a monster peak, it's a full-on catastrophe.

Not only were we going to go hungry, but I had spent the whole day lugging that damn hex burner up the hill for nothing.

But it was just about to get even worse.

We had set up camp on a slope; we had no choice; we were on the side of a mountain, after all. And although our makeshift tent had protected us from the rain coming at us vertically, the water was now starting to run down the hill, under the side of the tent, and starting to dampen our rucksacks and sleeping bags. Gently trickling its way through the grass, slowly edging its way downhill. We tried to divert it using our bags, but the trickle became a stream.

In the driving rain, we got back out from under the gazebo that Freddie was certainly not claiming credit for now. In my frustrated, somewhat deluded state, I mentally pinned all blame for this on Freddie. Under the hoods of our coats, we grabbed everything we could to fight off the elements. Shrubs, the few plants and bushes that survived at this height, anything that would help us. The rain came down harder. The surrounding mountains barely visible through the mist. Our plan, if you can call it that, was to replant these scrub-like bushes uphill and weave each branch through the uprights of the gazebo to try and divert the flow of water. We stood back to admire our work. It, just about, held. The water hit our makeshift fence and worked its way around, circumnavigating the Gazebo. Bear Grylls would have been proud.

We got back under, it was damp, sure, but at least we weren't sleeping in a river.

As we settled down again, we suddenly became very aware of how cold it was. We were hungry, wet, freezing (there was snow on the peaks around us) and seriously considered walking the 3-hour hike back to Audrey. Even if it was pitch dark.

I shivered incessantly, trying to wrap my arms around my body to stay warm. My sleeping bag helped, but I couldn't get dry. *We're going to be one of those campfire stories,* I thought to myself. I wasn't ready to panic just yet, but I was certainly on the way.

Mercifully, we made it through to 5 am, huddled together, drifting in and out of sleep, when the sun started to rise. I've never watched the sunrise from such altitude. As the sun peeked over the mountain range ahead, we were bathed in its warming glow whilst the valley below was still tucked up in darkness. Freddie and I lay there, trying to dry off, as we watched the light creep slowly down the mountain beneath our feet and then bound over the valley below. Sunrise over a mountain range gives the sunlight such a definite edge, like a torch in the night. We could watch the sunlight's progression over the landscape, each house, street, and field suddenly illuminated as morning arrived. For a short while, I forgot how cold and wet I was and just sat and watched.

We packed everything up and started the march back down the hill, head down in silence.

* * *

A dark cloud hung over us on the drive back to Tbilisi. The experience on the mountain scared us more than we would have liked to admit. I felt embarrassed more than anything. We were on such a high in Turkey, celebrating how much we had matured as travellers, learning from our mistakes. But yet again, we had screwed up, and what was more maddening than anything was that it was completely our own doing. We weren't caught in an unlucky accident. This was all on us.

My mind turned again to Central Asia. If we continued to mess up there, we might not be lucky enough to be embarrassed. We had to take things more seriously; we had to prepare. But I doubted our ability to do that. I know how easily we get carried away by new ideas. Given that tendency, perhaps we had bitten off more than we could chew. Not many words were spoken on that journey back; it was a journey of introspection.

When we arrived back to Tbilisi, we cheered ourselves up by watching the cricket in the only place that we could find that had Wi-Fi; McDonald's. We lost our composure when a wicket fell. But judging from the surprised reaction from our neighbouring Georgians, they're not huge cricket fans.

We split up to conduct some life admin. Freddie would head off to the post office to pick up Audrey's *original* ownership documents. Whereas I went to the Azerbaijani embassy to pick up our passports and freshly stamped visas. "No original. No entry!" Freddie cried as he departed in an extraordinarily poor Georgian accent.

I groaned as I arrived at the embassy; the queue snaked out of the door away from gesticulating officials. Shortly after taking my position in the queue, a distinctly European-looking man with blond hair and blue eyes joined behind me. Forgetting how to start a conversation, I turned my head and nodded at him in that awkward way you do when seeing a recognisable face in a foreign land.

"Christian," he said as he leaned towards me.

"Excuse me?" my heart sank with the realisation that I was going to have to choose between our visas or avoiding the advances of a Jehovah's Witness.

"My name. It's Christian," he said, holding out his hand.

"Oh, right!" I said with a relieved smile spreading across

my face. His name was actually Christiaan, and he was from Amsterdam, I learned as we made introductions and small talk.

"What were you doing in this part of the world?" I asked him.

"Oh, we're hitchhiking to Iraq," he replied as nonchalantly as if he was off down to the shops for a pint of milk.

Whilst we waited for our turn with the embassy official's visa stamp, he mapped out his route for me from Tbilisi to Baghdad. Realising their planned route actually followed ours for a good distance, I offered him a lift.

"Oh, you're driving?!" he said, not believing his luck. "In what? Do you have space for three?"

"Oh yeah," I replied, "We're in an ambulance; plenty of space," I replied, laughing at his reaction.

And so began one of the most entertaining and hell-raising legs of our trip.

Christiaan led me back to his hostel to meet with his two travelling companions. It turned out they had been trying to get a lift east out of Tbilisi for a week without success, so he was pretty excited to introduce me to the others.

"Boys, guess what?!" He shouted as stormed into their dorm room. "I have a lift, in the back of an ambulance!"

And with lots of handshaking, backslapping and relieved faces, I met Joost and Arjen, who made up the remainder of this unlikely trio. A journalist and two engineers, they had (like us) just graduated from University and were after one last thrill, "Before those corporate bastards take us for good!" as Arjen neatly put it, with a heavy Dutch accent.

They packed up their bags and followed me back to Audrey, where Freddie was waiting with the ownership documents.

"Where the fuck have you been?!" he welcomed. To be fair,

I had been three hours when I had promised a thirty-minute turnaround.

"I've found some friends!" I replied, "We're gonna take them to Baku!"

And with that, we shoved the Dutchies in the back, swinging from our hammocks as we headed east out of Tbilisi towards our next country, Azerbaijan.

These three Dutch men were putting us to shame. Whatever stupid and idiotic ideas that we could come up with, they could do in their sleep. Our stories of beatings and tent forgettings were not in the same stratosphere as the gleeful stupidity that they embarked upon. They were hitchhiking all the way to Iraq, for God's sake. It was just the kick we needed at the right time. Confidence restored.

As we set out towards the border, I could hear my dad saying, 'Just never, never take hitchhikers across borders, Max!'

We passed through what seemed to be the once industrial heartland of Georgia, the road east dissected a huge but now decaying steelworks that we imagined must have powered half the Soviet Empire from this forgotten corner. We got out for a look.

It was like a ghost town, with the remaining steel girders holding what was left of the buildings in place, hanging in a way that seemed to suggest they were resigned to their fate. Sagging down towards the earth, waiting for their final fall — like a man on death row — they'd been waiting too long, swinging off the few screws and bolts that kept them in place.

Their brothers and sisters, neighbouring bits of metal that had already made their final descent grew out of the long grass like zombies' hands bursting from a grave, beckoning the rest of the structure to fall too.

We looked around; it haunted the hell out of me. Walking around abandoned buildings, every creek of steel and crack of wood became the footsteps of a crazed murderer in my mind. And once it was in there, I couldn't shake it. Now the shadows were chasing me.

"Let's get out of here; it's giving me the creeps."

The short route from Tbilisi to the Azerbaijani border was the first taste of the roads to come. The Georgians were desperate to cosy up to Europe to protect themselves from the Russian Bear to the North. Nowhere was this clearer than the difference between the infrastructure of west and east. From the Turkish border to Tbilisi, you could have closed your eyes and, upon opening them, imagined you were in Switzerland. Perfectly smooth roads and green valleys. The east was a different story. As soon as you lost sight of the capital, you were plunged into a different world. The roads deteriorated, the earth was scorched, the industry rotting and the bridges that we planned to cross had fallen through.

Progress was painfully slow, but we made the border around 5 pm. As had now become standard practice, we camped at the border that night to give us a full day to cross the following morning.

One thing to know about Freddie and me is that we both have the music taste of seventy-year-old men. Unfortunately, however, the music tastes of a very different seventy-year-old. The first argument every morning would be who would be in charge of the playlist. Mine would be dominated by the Rolling Stones, the Beatles and Bob Dylan, or Freddie's, which had

Stevie Wonder, Genesis, or other unmentionable tripe.

So that night, we put it to Christiaan, Joost and Arjen whose playlist should we listen to? Fortunately, they had good taste, and The Beatles won out. I took great joy in that victory. So that night, we built a campfire, cooked up some local sausages, uncorked some of our remaining Georgian wine and belted out *Hey Jude*, *Penny Lane*, and *Yellow Submarine* into the early hours, gazing at impossibly bright stars. All was right with the world.

11

Azerbaijan

That morning we rose early and headed straight for the border, eager to avoid a repeat of our Georgian border crossing with our friend on the Segway.

Upon arriving, we were immediately separated. All passengers had to cross on foot, and only one person was allowed to stay with Audrey. That one person was me.

Westerners crossing between Georgia and Azerbaijan are few and far between, which served to heighten the border guards' senses and eyebrows.

Audrey was backed into a holding bay, and I was marshalled into a nearby building with a whitewashed interior, black leather furniture and official documents fluttering in the breeze from a groaning ceiling fan. After a short wait, I was sat down in front of a stern-looking man in his late 20's clothed in military fatigues and a matching cap. The camouflage struck me as being inappropriately green, halfway to turquoise, for protecting a country that was mostly desert. He also wore a marvellous glistening moustache, as any border guard worth his mustard east of the Iron Curtain does.

"Why are you driving through Azerbaijan?" straight to the point, ignoring any niceties as he stared down at my passport.

Realising it was game time, I sat up in my chair, trying to look respectable. "We're on the way to Beijing."

"What? Don't joke with me; I can make your life very tough."

"I promise you; I'm not joking. Look, we have all our visas."

He looked up at me with quizzical eyes, deciding whether to believe my story or not.

He shook his head and moved onto a new line of questioning "It's too hot in Azerbaijan; your English van will break down."

"Well, I hope not!" Realising I should have had a better answer as soon as the words left my mouth.

"Are you bringing any drugs into Azerbaijan? This is a very serious offence in my country."

I sat forward in my chair and said with as much conviction as I could muster, "No".

Looking me square in the eyes for a second time. "We will find them." He uttered slowly.

"I promise, no drugs," I said, catching myself scratching my nose and shuffling nervously from one side of the chair to the other. Looking about as convincing as a twenty-two-year-old reveller travelling from Bogota to Ibiza with nothing but a boogie board.

With an exhale of reluctance, he stamped my passport with unnecessary force and slid it back under the window. That bang-bang of pressing the stamp into the ink and then slamming it down onto an empty page of our passports became a sweet sound that signified our ordeal was nearly over.

Border guards carry out their stamping procedure with unnecessary force. Hammering down the stamp to symbolise their acceptance of your entry into their country. BANG BANG!

Whether you are in the US or Central Asia, the same is always true. Maybe it's their way of saying, "We mean business here; you had better not fuck around," or maybe it's just an ego thing. Either way, I've always found the men behind the window at international borders amongst the meanest and miserable you can encounter. They have an ability to make it seem like there is not a chance in hell that they are going to approve your entry right up until the moment they stamp your passport. It's the absolute contempt in their eyes when they look at your passport and then at you and the mock bewilderment greeting each of your answers to their questions. It's as if every border guard around the world goes to a special training camp to learn how to act in this way. As you can probably tell, I don't like border guards.

The answers I gave this particular border guard clearly didn't satisfy his curiosity, so he instructed his ground team to conduct a strip search of Audrey. He shouted his instructions in a blast of Azerbaijani that made everything sound much worse than it actually was. I told myself that, in any case.

Over the next forty minutes, they systematically pulled everything out of the back of Audrey. First to go were our camp beds, then our cooking equipment. This I could deal with. These big items could easily be put back. But then the bastards started rifling through our cupboards and draws, chucking our bandages, medicines, and ration packs over their shoulders as they went. One of the men fixed me with a glare and a smirk as he did so, not even bothering to look in the drawer he was dismantling.

These smaller items had taken weeks of trial and error to pack correctly. A small change in organisation would start an incessant rattling in the bowels of Audrey that would send a monk to despair.

I watched on in resignation as our possessions sailed through the air and landed in the dust beside me. My hands clenched in annoyance as I tried trying to stay as calm as possible. They would love nothing more than to provoke a reaction.

The first item that caused a bit of excitement was our cricket bat.

"What this!?" one of them shouted.

"It's a cricket bat," I tried to explain, showing them with a textbook forward defensive, which only confused the situation further.

It was met by the bafflement that anyone will be familiar with if they've tried to explain cricket to someone from a non-cricket-playing nation. "It lasts how long??" was usually the next reply.

It was such a shame Freddie wasn't with me; we could have given them a quick lesson. I would have loved to have whacked my friend, the stamp man, out of the ground over the Azerbaijani border. Perhaps it would have triggered the birth of a new cricket-playing nation. Alas.

After the interest around the cricket bat had died down, the next item to get them really excited was our axe. We had packed an axe to chop up firewood, always knowing it was going to get us into trouble at some point.

One of the men emerged from the back of Audrey with the axe raised triumphantly over his head, desperate to show his boss. His eyes shouting 'We've got them!'

I reluctantly agreed to throw out the axe, it was bound to happen at some point, I suppose. Although that was short change for Freddie when I tried to explain things on the other side. "I would have convinced them to let us keep it, easily," he later protested.

I got so exhausted and frustrated at border crossings. We had an unhappy knack of crossing in the heat of the day, and the borders would always be complete dust pans with no shade. They call Azerbaijan the land of fire, and they aren't joking. It's the hottest place I've ever been.

The next thing to come out were all our rucksacks, including the Dutchies' bags, who were safely waiting on the other side with Freddie.

Christ, I really hope they didn't bring any of their local produce, I thought to myself as the first of their bags were torn through. I chastised myself for not making them carry their own bags across the border. "Idiot," I muttered as my stress level rose. Anything could be in there.

As the second of their bags were torn through, suddenly everyone was called off; some more pressing matter had clearly materialised. A sense of relief rushed over me; we were good to go.

That is as soon as I had packed everything back into Audrey. Thanks, gents.

On his way out, one of the guards, seeing all the names of the people we had met on the back of the van, wanted to add his own. He drew a huge and remarkable Azerbaijani flag on the back of Audrey alongside a towering eagle, the national bird of Azerbaijan. Although thankful for his artwork, it must have taken him thirty minutes, with all the intricacies he insisted on adding to the wings and the beak of the bird, and it was breaching 40C. I just wanted to get out of this hellhole.

The guards opened up the gates of our quarantine area, and I drove across the border to whoops and high-fives from the

Dutchies, who had been waiting for over two hours. They had breezed through, of course.

Fred, meanwhile, had got himself into quite an excitable state. "Thank fuck for that," he said. It emerged that Joost had said he left a bit of weed in his bag that was in the van.

"You fucking did what?!" I screamed at him, with all the frustrations of a hot and stressful border crossing boiling over.

"I was joking, I was joking," he blurted back in a less than convincing tone.

I hadn't brushed up on my Azerbaijani drug trafficking rules recently, but I was fairly sure getting caught with the stuff would result in me rotting in some godforsaken sun-soaked jail for the rest of my days, or perhaps something grizzlier. I didn't press Joost any further; I wasn't sure I really wanted to know the answer in any case.

* * *

For anyone unfamiliar with this corner of the Caucasuses, let me bring you up to speed. A lot can be learned, as it often can, from the counties' access to oil from under their feet. And let me tell you, there is a silly amount of oil in Azerbaijan. The stuff just pours out of the ground. In actual fact, there's so much it you can go to a spa and lay in a bath of oil, and people do. Apparently, it cures impotence, but I wouldn't recommend it. At the turn of the twentieth century, Baku, the capital, produced more than half of the world's petroleum. So as you can imagine, there's a lot of money around and, as we would find out, an equal amount of corruption. If you had assumed this money had flowed down to those who needed it most, you'd be wrong.

Owing to this, the ruling elite are keen to hold onto power. The country is run by a man called Aliyev, who inherited the presidency from his dad, an impressive feat in a democracy. He is currently well into his third term even though when he was elected, there was a two-term maximum.

And just to dot the i's of this dictatorship, in all but name. His government certainly doesn't have a reputation for compassion and empathy. Beating or imprisoning anyone that dares to ask awkward questions about irrelevant matters such as democracy, corruption or, most irrelevant of all, human rights is widely encouraged.

Of course, these are all facts we've learnt subsequently.

* * *

Glad the border ordeal was over; we decided that the best thing would be to find some lunch, a cold beer and get out of this damn heat.

Everyone got back aboard, and we drove off into our twelfth country. As we left the compound, I noticed our mileometer read 5,495 miles. 5,500 would be our halfway point. We shouted each mile as it ticked over, getting the Dutchies involved as well.

"5,496...5,497...5,488...5,499...!

5,500!" We screamed in unison, high-fiving and ruffling

137

each other's heads. It felt like a huge moment; we were now closer to Beijing than we were to Oxford. It would be easier to keep going than turn back.

We pulled over at the first restaurant we came across. "Kafe" slapped across its face and surrounded by white plastic tables covered in plastic tablecloths emblazoned with garish bright pink hearts. The owner pulled out a chair from the table as we arrived, as he welcomed us with his other hand.

He didn't speak a word of English and mysteriously didn't have any menus either. Fortunately, we had already grasped "beer" in Russian, and five cold ones soon appeared. But the food aspect of the equation was much trickier. We resorted to a game of charades.

After making a fool out of ourselves trying to act out a kebab with all of us standing like a pencil with our hands above our heads and twirling around to try and mimic the turning kebab on the spit, a chicken ran between our legs. Freddie spotting our opportunity, immediately pointed at it, saying, "We'll have that, please!" I don't think he expected the proprietor to take him literally (we wanted chicken, but not necessarily that specific chicken) but the man picked up the poor bird and with one swoop of his arm, wrung its neck.

"Well, that's one way of doing it, I guess," said Christiaan as we sat there bemused.

The owner then suggested one chicken wasn't enough for all five of us. And despite our protests, he bent down, picked up one of its sisters and wrung her neck too.

We were too hungry to get ourselves too worried, and soon thereafter, a feast of fresh salad, bread and chicken tagine arrived with the most amazing tomato and herb sauce. Everything was in the pan; it felt like a biology class as we tried to decide what was the liver, heart, lungs, or something else entirely. It was delicious, and everything was eaten, bar a few organs, and along with drinks, the whole meal came to just £15 for the five of us. *We're going to enjoy Azerbaijan*, I thought.

* * *

Azerbaijan boasts the largest flag in the world, it's the size of a football pitch and my word, are they proud of it. They also used to have the largest flagpole in the world (naturally) until their neighbours across the Caspian Sea, Turkmenistan, in a fantastically immature piece of diplomatic one-upmanship, built one that was slightly bigger. This did not go down well. They also bloody love carpets. They even have a building in the capital shaped like a carpet. Google it; it's worth seeing.

We continued to Baku to heat rising and rising through the day. Without air conditioning, we'd resorted to driving with the windows down, which was only marginally better than driving with the windows up. The air so hot it felt like blasting a hairdryer directly into your face. It hurt to breathe.

But despite that, spirits were high, and we were halfway through our first afternoon rendition of *Hey Jude* when our bubble was burst as we were marshalled off the road, and so began the play described in the first chapter of this book.

Freddie, up a Georgian mountain

Halfway along the Jvari Pass

12

Police

It's worth pausing to give you context on the local constabulary in this part of the world. The police force in Azerbaijan and, as we were to discover, the rest of Central Asia are not publicly funded. They're private organisations.

This means two things:

- Firstly: they have the freedom to be vicious bastards with no politicians to answer to. Roughing up a few tourists results in few ramifications.
- Secondly: without public funding, they need to make money in other ways. One of their primary sources of income were fines; the other was bribes.

Our run-in outside Ganja described in the opening chapter of this book was our first, but it certainly wouldn't be our last. We racked up driving convictions on a daily basis. Whenever

Audrey came trundling around a corner, English number plate glistening in the sun, any copper worth their brass wanted to bust us by any means available. Whether their resulting "charges" were based on anything factual, we would soon learn, was a secondary concern, if that.

Our charges included:

- Bog-standard speeding (the police officer would rarely have a speed gun but judge our speed "by eye" which was apparently completely legitimate).
- Driving on the wrong side of the road (we were overtaking a horse).
- Drunk driving (they found an unopened bottle of wine in the back of the van).
- And my favourite of all, scaring a camel (this is not a joke).

Often they wouldn't even bother with an offence, they would just hustle you for $10 for simply being in the wrong place at the wrong time.

It's difficult to reason with a man who is completely unconcerned with whether the offence he has charged us with has any grounding legally or factually.

"This is a very serious offence in my country," they would say in heavy Russian accents, looking at us with a level of seriousness that would have just about been merited if we had been caught stealing the nation's oil reserves. Which, I can assure you, would be *a very serious offence in this country.*

When we were charged with these offences, we had two

options. We could either wait it out until they got bored of us, which would take anything from two to six hours. Or we could just pay the fine, which we often did.

Choosing to pay the fine would give us the opportunity to negotiate. But, as we found to our detriment, negotiating a bribe was like walking a tightrope, any misstep and they've got you for bribing a public official, which was (all together now) "a very serious offence in this country."

But by the time we left Central Asia, we had our act nailed. It would go something like this:

The policeman would make it clear that whatever minor offence you had or had not just committed was a very serious offence in his country and the best you could hope for was life imprisonment, if you were lucky.

Over to Freddie and I.

"Salaam-Alaikum, Salaam-Alaikum!" (God be with you), we would shout as we shook everyone's hands. There would be anywhere between three and fifteen officers at each post and often various distant relatives who had dropped in to see the show, all of which would want to clasp both hands around ours. As such, this procedure could take some time. All the while, we tried to be as chirpy and unperturbed as possible.

Then the inspection of Audrey would begin. Suspicions high to begin with; a trundling British Ambulance was not an everyday occurrence in this forgotten corner of the world after all. However, sniggers would soon break out when they saw some of the drawings and names on the back. "Ah, Dimitry!" they'd point and laugh whilst shaking their heads, recognising the name of a colleague who had swindled us a few miles earlier. Things at this stage would be relatively jovial and friendly. Lots of back-slapping and the like.

We would then be taken to their station, be offered copious amounts of tea, and be sat down opposite the head honcho who would always have a perfectly circular belly straining at his shirt buttons, always have a well-groomed moustache, and always have a cap that just about squeezed onto bulging his head with beads of sweat glistening at the creases. This final detail seemed like a significant mark of authority, and these standards were dutifully upheld from Baku to Ulaanbaatar.

Suddenly the atmosphere would change. The boss would read aloud from a piece of paper that had just been put in front of him (which certainly had nothing to do with us, given the time it would take to compose a report of such length). He would shake his head and mutter something to a few of his colleagues over this shoulder, drop the paper on his desk and lean back into his chair in a resigned fashion and rub his eyes beneath his glasses.

"This is a very serious offence, in my country." (You guessed it).

Taking off his glasses and slowly cleaning each lens, he would continue. "I'm sorry, it's out of my hands. There's nothing I can do for you now." Raising his glasses to inspect them in the light.

We'd be worried if we hadn't heard those words three times today already.

"It's a shame because I like you, my friend" (We'd just met him).

This would be the signal to open up negotiations.

"Surely there is something you can do; think of all the paperwork," we'd retort.

"Ha!" he would laugh, "I do hate paperwork." Flashing a

look at colleagues as if to say, "we've got a live one here!"

"But I don't know, this is a very serious offence in my country," he wasn't going to give up easily.

They would then speak amongst each other in Russian for what would seem like an eternity. Almost certainly just talking about the football, the weather, anything other than us.

He would then turn back.

"Okay, I've tried really hard; we really like you guys, so we can make this go away. But...There is an administrative cost. You know, for all the paperwork." He would say, whilst looking out of the window.

"Okay, how much?"

He'd take a deep breath. "One thousand US Dollars," as he exhaled.

They would always start ridiculously high.

This is where the dance would begin. This was our favourite part.

"Ha!" We would reply, "Who carries a thousand US dollars around with them!?" Showing mock bafflement, Freddie and I exchanged glances. We'd maybe throw in something a little extra here, like throwing up our arms in exasperation or feigning spitting out our tea.

The inflation in most Central Asian countries was so high that paying for a meal would quite literally involve the transfer of a small bag of cash, so to have $1,000 on you would involve several support cars.

Which, of course, they knew.

Now, the key trick (which we learnt the hard way) was to agree on an amount first and then hand over the cash. If you just hand over the cash, that's when they would get you. With a flicker of a smile, you'd know you've fallen into their trap and be charged with the bribery of a public official, making this game an expensive one. But we were no longer amateurs, no sir.

We would counteroffer with a healthy discount. "How about 5 dollars".

It was now their turn to feign complete derision. Arms thrown in the air, backs were turned, and they'd threaten to walk away from negotiations.

The key here was to stay wholly straight-faced and not to react to all their damning warnings about the future of our lives in some squalid jail in the desert or their wild gesticulations. Just. Stay. Calm.

"Oh, you've pushed it too far now. There is nothing we can do for you. Call the army! You will spend the rest of your days with an Iranian as a boyfriend. You like this?! Huh! You know what those Iranian pigs will do to you!"

Our prospective boyfriends wouldn't always be Iranian. Sometimes they were Afghani, sometimes Uzbek. Whoever was the neighbouring nation at the time. It was the Afghani boyfriends that we had to be particularly careful of, it seemed. They seemed to be big fans of young Englishmen in jail cells, judging by the excitement of our captors as they reeled off their stories.

Eventually, after a series of back-and-forth offers, they would either get bored of us or realise they're never going to get through.

An agreement would be reached, usually in the region of $10-$20. The more experience we got, the more we refined our strategy, and the cheaper it got.

As soon as the payment was made, the atmosphere would immediately change; we were all best mates again. More tea would flow, cigarettes were offered, sometimes, we would even be invited back to their family home for lunch. And we would always have a picture with their entire family in front of Audrey. It was truly bizarre.

A few more parting *Salaam-Alaikums*, and we would drive off. A complete charade.

We kept count of the number of times we were pulled over in such a fashion. Freddie got pulled over twenty times in Uzbekistan alone.

But despite all the handshakes, *Salaam-Alaikums* and back-slapping, I always had the feeling that we just had to run into one bad'un and that was it. Even though we got better and better at handling these situations, I always approached those men with a deep pain in my stomach. Someone told us before we left that the only people we need to be scared of in central Asia were the policemen; they were dead right.

The Central Asian police, in differing
standards of attire

Border guards signing the back of Audrey,
after deciding we weren't smuggling drugs

13

Baku

Our second run-in with the law came on the same day as the first. As we made our way to Baku, we were pulled over by a kid who looked no more than sixteen with a AK47 pressed to his hip.

Clearly still in training, he took a more direct approach to his swindling, simply rubbing his thumb and forefinger together in our faces, the international sign of "Give me your fucking money," no crime even suggested.

It is interesting, the person holding the gun in these situations was always the youngest. Just a kid usually, who in some way probably loved standing around with a gun pointing at people like Freddie and I. Being only twenty-one ourselves, I could certainly resonate with his pride. But his youth only made me more nervous; I could see in his eyes that he couldn't yet fully comprehend the consequence of pulling the trigger on which his finger was twitching. Or perhaps I hadn't yet comprehended that there would be no consequence. Either way, I'd come to the conclusion, on balance, that giving AK47s to teenagers was a bad idea.

Fred, still in an irritated state of mind from being bent over by his colleague up the road, was in no mood. He put his foot down and left the teenager in our dust cloud whilst screaming profanities back at them through the open window.

To be pulled over twice within an hour convinced us that our third might not be so lucky. We agreed to keep our heads down until we hit the coast.

It's easy to make light of countries on the other side of the world arming teenagers. Being born in a land that has enjoyed stable sovereignty for several centuries is a privilege. Like a lot of the Middle East and Central Asia, the cause of the undercurrents of feeling and resentment in Azerbaijan are complex and nuanced. Azerbaijan, or at least the land on which Azerbaijan now sits, has been passed around like a hot potato over centuries between Russia to its north, Iran to its south and, more recently, Armenia to its west. Spilling into a potent cultural mix of Muslims, Russians, and Armenians, which often boils up to bloodshed. Having declared sovereignty from the Soviet Union in 1992, this was Azerbaijan's latest crack at independence and many were unhappy with that. Particularly the Armenians who, through no choice of their own, now find themselves living in a country that is not their own. All of which goes some way to explain the twitching finger on the trigger of the AK47 before me.

With every mile, the scenery would brighten and with it too the faces of the locals. The scenery began completely dry and scorched by the beating sun, nothing grew in these parts, and as we drove through the few scattered towns and villages, you could see on the faces of their inhabitants that life was tough. But the ground slowly changed from brown to a flourishing green and suddenly smiles and designer sunglasses appeared on the faces of the locals as we hit the coast and with it, Baku, Azerbaijan's capital.

Baku was an extraordinary place, buoyed by its oil-rich surroundings; it has a touch of Paris about it. With wide boulevards, designer outlets and the wealth needed to shop at such places it stands in jarring contrast to the rest of the country.

Towering above oil barons with expensive tastes was Baku's most famous and impressive sight, the Flame Towers. Inspired by Azerbaijan's nickname, The Land of Fires, these three towers lick their way into the skyline and dominate the view from whichever way you look. At the base of the towers was a Lamborghini shop.

The powers that be have done a particularly bad job of distributing the wealth generated by their oil bonanza. We'd only driven 200 miles that day, but it felt like we had crossed centuries. Mud huts to Lamborghinis in just over three hours.

Although I would have loved to put our morals to one side and bask in the luxury that Baku offered, we had a significant date at the port that would dictate the success of the whole trip. It was there that we were due to board the mythical ferry to Turkmenistan.

It was at this point we also had to say goodbye to our Dutch companions, Christiaan, Joost and Arjen. They were heading south to Iran, where we had been refused entry, and then onto Iraq. So, after a few photos and the customary signing of Audrey's rear end, we bid them goodbye. They had made a fleeting but sizeable impact on our trip. I have never met three people with such an amazing ability to throw caution to the wind in search of an adventure. It was a thoroughly refreshing chance encounter, and worked to shake ourselves out of the rut we'd been in since returning from the mountains. At a moment when we were having a crisis of confidence, they inspired us to keep going. After all, nothing we could do would be as stupid as hitch-hiking to Iraq.

I never did fully understand why they were hitchhiking to Iraq; they would just respond with a shrug and a "why not?" in their thick Dutch accent. But then again, we would get some equally puzzled looks when explaining why we were driving to Beijing.

* * *

Baku's port was a throng of activity, kept busy servicing nearby oil wells off the coast and pulling in tonnes of the Caspian Sea's world-famous caviar.

Ever since having to divert our route after being denied entry into Iran, we had placed all our chips on being able to cross the Caspian Sea on a lorry ferry that left once a week from this port and sailed across the Caspian to Turkmenbashi, a port city in Turkmenistan. The trip across took a mere twenty-four hours. However, we couldn't find any information on which day of the week or what time the ship would leave, and everyone at the port was similarly out of the picture.

After driving around the port for some time, we finally found the right office for this particular enterprise. We were greeted by a colossal Russian built like a brick house; he had broad shoulders and bulbous features. He was dressed in soiled overalls and a frayed checked shirt. Our timing was unfortunate — we had interrupted his dinner. He stood up, visibly annoyed, and mopped away the grease of whatever unfortunate being had served as his food with his oil-stained sleeve. He made no effort to show any interest in our plight.

Taking one look at Audrey, he flatly refused our offer of custom. Only commercial lorries were allowed, he said.

Fuck.

However, his stance loosened after slipping him $10 (we were learning). He said he would see what he could do. Which meant that if, when the next ship was full, and they couldn't fit any more lorries, but there was room for Audrey, we would be in luck.

"When would that be?" we asked.

He met this with a shrug of his shoulders. "When the ship is full."

It turned out that the way this operation worked was the patient lorry drivers would form a queue as they arrived at the port, and when that queue reached a certain size, they would fill up the ferry and sail off. No matter whether it was 5 pm or 2 am. Or on Thursday or Tuesday. The ferry would leave and without much warning. Sometimes this would take a day, sometimes a week. It just depended on the traffic.

This put us in an awkward position. One of us would have to be awake at all times to make sure the ship didn't leave without us. So, we started shift work. Six hours on, six hours off, guarding our position in the queue. Fortunately, Freddie drew the short straw and took the first night on watch.

We paid our dues to the still-slobbering Russian, which were calculated on Audrey's length. Coincidentally, Audrey's length pushed her just over from the bloody expensive category to the exorbitantly expensive category. I think that had more to do with us interrupting his dinner than anything to do with Audrey's berth.

We offered to further grease his palm with enough money to take whichever poor soul had agreed to be his wife out for dinner, in order to reduce the fee, but this time he refused. Which just about wiped out our remaining US dollars. I hope they would have cash points in Turkmenistan.

And so, the wait began. Fortunately, this turned out to be one of the main trade routes connecting the West to Afghanistan, and the queue quickly formed behind us with lorries carrying aid and supplies to rebuild the country our government had spent the last two years unbuilding.

I settled down into a deck chair to try and get some sleep. At around 4 am I awoke to the shriek of the ferry's horn, I jumped up to find all the lorries that had topped and tailed us, gone. And Freddie, who was meant to be on night watch, snoring in his chair beside me. I kicked him awake as I ran down the jetty, relieved to find our Russian with the ramp still down.

"You're in luck! We have space. Welcome to the Grandmother," he shouted in a thick Russian accent as I approached.

"Why is it called the Grandmother?" I replied.

"The oldest ship in our fleet," he laughed as he proudly gazed over her like you might look at a dog who was well beyond her years, but still somehow stumbling along.

That was not what I needed to hear.

The Grandmother was one of seven ageing Soviet relics that plied this route. These now rusting hulks were designed to bridge the gap between the fertile and green Caucasus region and the arid but populated cities of central Asia. The trade route was once a vital source of food for Stalin's disciples. Once.

As Freddie and I drove Audrey down towards the gangway and set eyes on the Grandmother, it was clear that there had been no investment since Stalin's death.

I don't know much about the Soviet Union. But I do know it didn't end well. And I can't help but feel that when they were auctioning off their assets, health and safety wasn't a pressing concern.

It wasn't so much her age, but her design that worried us the most. She was unnaturally tall and narrow, like a boat that was designed for a canal rather than open water. If you imagine a standard car ferry, the Grandmother was just as long and tall, but only half as wide. The sight of her gave an unnerving sense of instability. She lay there moored against the harbour, swaying from side to side with the tide like a drunk duck.

We later learnt that her precarious balance wasn't just a figment of our imagination. Just five years earlier, one of the Grandmother's daughters got caught in a storm and capsized, killing all but seven of her passengers. All they've done since to improve the safety of the vessels following this disaster is to limit the number of passengers the ships can take, thus reducing the number of lives lost in future disasters. Smart.

Our first ordeal was the gangplank. Instead of your usual nice and wide ferry gangplank offering a simple gentle incline, the ferry had two thin boards, one for each wheel, offering you a route from the safety of the land into the belly of the monster. Via several heart-stopping moments 100 metres above the Caspian. Getting the right line was critical.

We hesitated and stopped before we reached the gangplank. A man beside the ship saw our concern and kicked awake his three mates, who could sense an opportunity for profit.

Quick as a flash, they were up on their feet, marshalling us over as if they were directing a jumbo jet to its gate.

Lots of shouting and waving did little to convince us of the safety of the operation, but thankfully with Freddie driving, he put Audrey into first, and we slowly crept towards the two ramps.

Our new friends didn't inspire confidence. At any one moment, two of our unwanted helpers would be beckoning us over to the right, whilst the other two would be pointing left. We mostly ignored them, but if a consensus did appear, and it rarely did, we would heed their warning and turn hard in the way they were pointing.

The heat of the night did little to ease our stress. Two wheels, thank god, met the gangplank as one and, slowly, we eked up the incline.

"Don't look down, don't look down!" I whispered to myself.

I looked down. Only to see the surface of the Caspian reflecting the moonlight back at us, licking up the side of Grandmother, beckoning us down. Freddie, hands sweating, held the wheel as tightly as he could to pass the chasm and not let either of the wheels slip off the edge.

With two wheels on the plank, our helpful friends clearly thought their work was done and went to sit back down. Abandoning us at the most perilous moment.

We crept forwards, with the angle of the incline pushing us back into our seats.

After what felt like an eternity, Audrey's front tyres touched down on the deck, Freddie accelerated, and we were home and dry. Well, not quite; we now had twenty- four hours on this damned vessel.

We were ushered to a tight spot between two lorries carrying their wares into Asia. As soon as we opened the doors, we were met by the master of our little gang, who had helped us onto the ferry requesting his dues. On the little sleep we had, handing over a few notes seemed like a much better deal than an argument. Off he went to distribute his winnings amongst his friends. Leaving us to walk — or rather stumble — with the sway of the boat, clutching for anything that would break our fall, up the stairs in search of our cabin. Audrey was left to tackle this challenge on her own.

The bedrooms were only bedrooms because someone said they were. In our damp, squalid, and outrageously hot room were two single beds with a mattress each, and that's where the good news stopped.

There were no sheets, and the previous prisoner had clearly not bothered to bring his own. There was no further furniture, the only other feature of the room was the tiniest of portholes that let in the bare minimum amount of air. The air outside was north of 40 degrees, so whether you wanted to let it in any way was another case entirely.

There was a bathroom, but before we got too excited about having our first shower for three days, we turned the tap on. The water came out in a rust-tinged dribble and the bath, with a suspicious red tinge, was almost certainly the scene of a murder that hadn't been investigated.

We retreated back to the galley. We wouldn't be sleeping in our cabin that night, that's for sure.

The galley didn't offer anything better. It seemed that all the rooms were the same, as our fellow inmates had come to the same conclusion and were setting up their quarters in the communal area. Clearly, we were the only newbies on onboard as we had missed out on the rush to grab a spot. Hundreds of lorry drivers heading back to Afghanistan, the modern-day silk traders, were draped across the floor. No room left at the inn.

The soundtrack to the room was arguments and spitting. Summoning up long-lost pieces of phlegm that were happily living at the bottom of their stomach with an outrageous spine-shuddering noise. Our shipmates would then launch it across the room at considerable speed and with little remorse.

I couldn't bear it. Each spit and argument reverberated around my sleep-deprived brain. We continued to look elsewhere for comfort. Driven by a lack of other options, we climbed up onto the roof of the Grandmother, where we found some space and privacy. It certainly wasn't designed for it, but this would have to do. Lying on the steel roof between two chuntering chimneys, with a gentle sea breeze cooling our aching bodies, we finally found rest for the first time in days and slept.

From what I can understand, nobody can make their mind up as to whether the Caspian is a sea or the world's largest lake. It's circumnavigated by land and doesn't directly feed into an ocean, the key characteristics of a lake, but it's filled with salt water. And although it doesn't sound like it, this classification actually matters.

There is a huge wealth of oil and gas under the Caspian's bed. Some estimate up to 48 billion barrels of oil, which is comfortably more than the rest of the world's oil fields produce each year, and 8.3 trillion cubic meters of natural gas, which is over double the annual output of the rest of the world. Rendering the area one of the most strategically important on the planet. The sea-cum-lake is surrounded by Kazakhstan to the northeast, Russia to the northwest, Azerbaijan to the west, Iran to the south, and Turkmenistan, our eventual destination, to the southeast. All of whom want to get their hands on its valuable produce.

Here's why it matters. If the powers at be decide it's a lake, the oil reserves will be divided up equally. Whereas if they decide it's a sea, all bets are off, and scuffles will likely ensue. In 2018 a decision was finally reached after two decades of arguing. After much thought and no doubt lobbying, it was decided that it was neither. Which helped no one and ensured the water of the Caspian will likely boil up to be a global concern in the not-too-distant future.

To add to the tensions, demand for its other prize product, Caspian caviar, which once accounted for 90% of all caviar sold around the world, has dropped off a cliff. Ethically focused shoppers have realised that the fishermen of the Caspian, who we are now watching in front of us chasing sturgeon in crude wooden boats, were catching the fish only to cut open their bellies, pull out their roe sacks and chuck them back in to die. I don't suspect it will be long before the governments of the competing nations clamour to replace that income with the black gold beneath the Caspian's waters.

I had initially seen the sheet-flat water of the Caspian as a blessing. At least the Grandmother wouldn't capsize, I thought. But the flat water meant no wind to carry the heat away. We woke with stiff necks from our makeshift steel pillows and had to hastily retreat to the phlegm fight that was the galley, cursing every time we touched bare metal.

With every creak of her undercarriage, the Grandmother edged towards our destination at a frustratingly slow pace.

And with each creak, the temperature rose and rose. We had no way of telling how hot it was, but it was stifling. All there was to do was to sit, wait and lose control of your emotions.

We moved back and forth between the deck and our cabin in search of some breeze but with no luck. We resigned ourselves to huddling in the main galley with everyone else. They were mostly made up of lorry drivers, largely Afghans who didn't give us the warmest of welcomes (understandably, considering our government's current exploits in their homeland). We slumped ourselves in the corner, trying to avoid their glares or their phlegm.

I caught eyes with the man to my left, "Where were you from?" I asked.

I was expecting him to shoot me a confused look and turn away.

But he replied, "Kabul."

I blushed.

"Have you been caught up in the war?"

"Yes"

"In what way?"

"My house, rocket", and he motioned an explosion with his hands and sad eyes. "Father, dead."

I felt trapped in the conversation, not knowing what to say. I let the silence hang in the air.

"Was it an American rocket?" Searching for a way out of the guilt and awkwardness.

He shrugged his shoulders and fiddled with something on the ground. When an unmanned drone hits your house, I guess you don't really care about the nationality of the finger that triggered it.

My eyes tried to catch someone else to break the silence.

Stumbling through the encounter. Babar, a cricket-loving Pakistani lorry driver with okay English, came to my rescue. We wound away the hours chatting about the recent exploits of the Pakistani cricket team, but my thoughts were still with the Afghani to my left, replaying the conversation over and over, each time coming up with something better to say than the awkward silence. I wanted to tell him that there was no public support for the war, that it was just politicians being politicians, but I never mustered the courage.

Babar, meanwhile, was chattering along happily. "We were robbed in that series! The umpires were bribed!" was a brief summary of his thoughts on Pakistan's recent tours of England and Australia.

And so passed the next twenty-four hours, trying to sleep, trying to keep cool — both equally unsuccessful — trapped in the steel underbelly of the drunkenly unstable Grandmother lurching from side to side.

The only manageable part of the day was at dusk, when we watched the sunset over the Caspian from the upper deck, a magical sight. The sun carried a deep orange, almost red colour there, and we bathed in the relative coolness that sunset ushered in.

Twenty-four sweat-soaked hours later, we arrived at the port of Turkmenbashi, so named after the President (read dictator) of Turkmenistan who gave himself that name. Roughly translated as "Leader of all Turks." As we'll learn, he's a down-to-earth sort of bloke.

14

Turkmenistan

Touching down on Turkmenistan's shores represented a major milestone on our journey: our entrance into Central Asia.

The vast area of land is made up of a group of Asian republics that were devised by Stalin to prevent a united Muslim bloc in his empire. Post-Soviet meltdown, they have been split into five countries that you would only have heard about during the news preceded by, "Three dissidents have been killed in..." or on the opening ceremony of the Olympics. So let me introduce you to the countries residing in this forgotten corner of the world; meet Tajikistan, Turkmenistan, Kyrgyzstan, Kazakhstan and Uzbekistan.

These forgotten nations stretch all the way from the Caspian Sea and Iran in the West to Mongolia and China in the East, and in doing so form a dividing line between the Islamic nations of the Middle East and the booming developing nations of eastern Asia. They form a potent mix of Islam, oil, and enough radioactive waste to terrify the rest of the world. China, Russia, and the US were all vying for power and control over these mismatched states but more importantly to me and Freddie;

they presented our only route forward.

Blocked by the soaring Himalayas to the south and the freezing desolation of Siberia to the north, this mix of cultures and religions loosely assembled into countries was our only bet on reaching China. We planned to take a northeastern route starting in Turkmenistan, crossing into Uzbekistan and then north through Kazakhstan, which would put us within striking distance of China.

Central Asia is one of the least visited places on earth, and Turkmenistan is the least visited of the lot, only getting 9,000 visitors a year (the UK beats that in an hour).

Turkmenistan is a victim of its geography. They find themselves within swinging distance of the Russians, who first got a taste of invading in 1717 and haven't kicked the habit since. Most recently, of course, it was the Soviet Union who came knocking and tucked them under their umbrella. They had grand plans but ended up using the country as their backyard, where they could dump anything from nuclear waste to awkward political opponents without the world seeing.

Similar to Azerbaijan, since finally gaining independence, Turkmenistan has fallen into the grasp of men with a zeal for ignoring presidential term limits, and the country has become one of the world's great dictatorships.

Following the dismantling of the Soviet Union, the country was ruled by Saparmurat Niyazov, who quickly renamed himself "Leader of all Turks." That's his official, legal name. He also retitled his position "President for Life", something which many dictators have achieved by suggestion, but few have done so literally. He's a classic dictator of the old school. Let me take you through his highlight reel.

He renamed all the days of the week and months of the year after members of his family. Suddenly, everyone had to stop saying, "I was born in March," and instead say ", I was born in Gurbansoltan", who was Niyazov's mother. Best of all, he renamed Monday after his mother-in-law. Why? Because everyone hates Mondays.

Now that he was warmed up, he banned opera, gold teeth and Spandex. No one knows why. He even named a crater on the moon after himself.

Next to go were black cars. You're not allowed to own a black car in Turkmenistan, as he believed they brought bad luck.

He then banned all newscasters from wearing makeup as he decided he couldn't tell male and female news presenters apart, which made him feel uncomfortable. And on the subject of media, he wrote a book. In order to ensure its success, he not only suppressed the release of all other books, but he mandated it required reading at all schools in the country, including driving schools. The book is about horses.

He then built golden statues of himself in every town and village he could find. The statues would either portray him proudly sitting astride a magnificent horse, or

standing in his suit, arms wide, as if to say, "bring it on." Some of the finer examples would continuously rotate so that he was always facing the fun.

Finally, he built a huge ski resort at great cost to the public purse. Not such a bad idea, perhaps, if you ignore the fact that it doesn't snow in Turkmenistan.

Although this makes entertaining reading, there is, of course, a more sinister side to this outrageous display of egotism. It was estimated that all these projects came at the cost of 50% of Turkmenistan's GDP annually. Read that again. Not 50% of the country's tax bill, 50% of its GDP. So, while he was running around the country creating monuments to himself, his people suffered. Since the Soviets left, there has been a steady decline in educational and health services, and nothing highlights this better than the fact that the authorities had to close every hospital outside of the capital due to a lack of public funds. I wonder how many hospitals that ski resort would have funded.

There were copious reports of food shortages across the country. However, they are very hard to verify as, unsurprisingly, the press has little freedom to report on such matters. The annual press freedom index ranked Turkmenistan 178th out of 180 countries, narrowly pipped to the post by Eritrea and North Korea. The only media outlet is controlled by the president, so even if someone was brave enough to run against him, they would have no way to communicate with the people. The Foreign Policy Centre recently described Turkmenistan as "teetering on the edge of catastrophe." Fortunately, Niyazov has died since our visit. But his position was quickly filled by a local dentist who, by all accounts, isn't much better.

And so, it was with trepidation that we stepped off the ferry. Relieved to be on solid ground but not entirely sure what to expect. Judging by the number of Afghans kneeling down to pray and kiss the earth, we weren't the only ones relieved to be off the Grandmother. It was late, so we camped at the port. I didn't yet have the stomach for the roads at night.

We woke up to find the Karakum Desert stretched out in front of us in all her glory.

We stepped out of Audrey to take in the full scope. It was an awesome sight. I'd never been to a proper desert, not really. And this didn't disappoint.

A childhood spent reading about Lawrence of Arabia came flooding back. I could just imagine him and his army appearing over the fold of a distant dune.

It's the emptiness that astounded me, the silence. There's nothing. The sky was clear, the air hot, and my gaze interrupted by nothing but the flicker of the heat and the odd rolling weed. Just dunes of sand for as far as the eye could see.

I immediately understood why so many travellers have been drawn to the romance of the Arabian desert; it nags at your curiosity.

"Come on, let's go see what's behind that dune," I said to Freddie, "or actually, what about THAT dune! Look at the size of it! "

After plenty of puffing and getting bogged down in deep sand, we got to the top of THAT dune and there was nothing, just like the others. But then, we thought, what about the next dune? Or the one after that? Before we knew it, we were a mile away from Audrey with no water, the mercury rising north of 40C, and we had lost half of one of the three good days of driving it was going to take to cross this inhospitable landmass.

We retreated back to Audrey and got out the map to look at what lay before us. There was one major road in this country and no other. Fortunately, it headed east. To its north, desert. To its south, mountains. The road planners had clearly learnt from experience that optionality was not a valued commodity when crossing a desert. You just want to get in and get out as soon as possible — no room for hanging around and certainly no room for getting lost.

Due to our visas, we had to cross this vast expanse of sand in three days flat. We would have to drive hard and fast and not look back. From the map, we reckoned it was about six hundred kilometres to Ashgabat, Turkmenistan's capital which was an oasis in the desert and the halfway point. About two days' drive on these roads and this heat, we thought. From there, we would plunge back into the desert and onto Uzbekistan.

Of course, the Western-bred worry inside of us set off all the usual alarms. Could we drive on these roads? What happens if we break down? Who will save us? Is it safe to camp out in the desert? WHAT ABOUT SNAKES!

The tingling mixture of fear and anticipation was controlling our minds.

When we started the trip, we had always planned to get this far; of course, we did. But at the same time, it seemed so unlikely that we actually would; it never seemed pertinent to plan the specifics until we got there.

So now that we were actually here, we didn't really know what to do. Driving across a desert with no fuel or water stops for 600km required a degree of forward planning that wasn't necessary in Europe.

So in a rare moment of responsibility, we made up some ground rules. We had two spare ten-litre containers of water, each would last us around two days if rationed, much less if the radiator overheated. Our rule was simple; we would never let our water supplies drop into the second supply tank.

Unfortunately, the water couldn't just be bought from a local 7/11. We'd source water from local wells and streams coming off the oases which then needed to be treated by dropping a chlorine pill in the top and waiting six hours. The resulting water tasted like you were drinking straight from a swimming pool on a warm summer's day.

Secondly, fuel. You don't want to run out of fuel out here. We had two jerry cans that would hold around a quarter of a tank each. Again, our rule was not to ever get into the final tank.

We filled every available container with spare water and diesel and set off.

As Freddie drove, I cracked open our previously unopened Lonely Planet guidebook. The first sentence read: "Only the deeply unfortunate or the clinically insane find themselves in Turkmenistan in July or August." The date? 28th July — we could not have timed it more perfectly.

In short order, we found out why. By nine o'clock, it was stiflingly hot; it literally hurt to breathe. The air boiled in your throat, and the wind was full of sand. We stopped off in a small village to buy what we would come to value like gold. Frozen bottles of Fanta. They were sold throughout Central Asia, and for those glorious first few sips, the near-frozen syrup provided relief from the heat. After two minutes, it had all thawed, and after three, it burnt you when you picked it up. The key was was to drink them fast and often. We would stop off in every town we could to buy refills for those thirty seconds of relief. It's a miracle we didn't turn orange.

Getting out of the van and into the shop was an exercise in itself. We would open our doors, count to three and then make a run for it, cursing under the heat of the midday sun until we made it to the cool shade of the shop, where we'd burst through the door to the bemusement of the proprietor.

The first village we stopped at was no more than a collection of mud huts. When you think of mud huts, you might immediately think the inhabitants were poor. But these guys were certainly not poor — not in the wider sense of the word. All they were doing was using local materials to build their houses. Just the way a Norwegian might use wood and an Englishman might use brick and stone; they use mud and sand. What's the difference?

As we left the shop, hugging gloriously cool bottles of Fanta, one of the locals stepped out of his hut into the midday sun and welcomed us with a smile the size of the Caspian. *Salaam-Alaikums* were exchanged, and he motioned with his arm to come inside.

The construction of the huts had a huge benefit. Inside they were cool, so gloriously cool. It was like teleporting from the heat of summer to the cool breeze of spring.

The sand from the desert was mixed through the mud like glitter, and when the sun shone, as it always did, it gave them a golden hue like a series of Buddhist temples glistening in the sun.

Teas were offered and refused and then offered again. Hot tea was the last thing I felt like, but it felt rude to reject their hospitality. Not much was said, but plenty of smiles were exchanged. We developed total admiration for the Turkmenis. Never had we come across such unmotivated generosity and such ability to turn the simplest things into things of wonder.

Ashamedly, after a while, I found the lack of speech awkward. It shouldn't have been. But we made our excuses, and after yet more Salaam-Alaikums we stepped back out into the sun.

It was comfortably the most uncomfortable place I had ever been, one shop surrounded by five mud huts and then nothing but desert. It was like living on Mars. The sands of the desert blended into the village like a sea lapping at its shores. No doubt the tide would rise at some point. The chickens — one of the few animals that seem to be able to stand the heat for longer than thirty seconds — seemed to love it. Perfect conditions for a dust bath in the dry soil. They pecked around incessantly, running back to the shade when their feet got too hot.

As we left the village, we drove past a thermometer, which seemed odd to start with — to see a large digital thermometer in such a place — but on rationalisation, the temperature was a serious issue there. In winter it can get down -33C and in summer comfortably over 50C. The reading screamed 53 degrees Centigrade in bold red letters.

It was Freddie's turn to drive, and I took over the redundant position of map reader and DJ. I stared ahead down the straight road, losing focus and allowing my thoughts to drift off in the pleasant way they do when you're being driven. I jolted back into consciousness when something interrupted the shimmers on the horizon.

"Is that a..." I said, pointing to the horizon, "no, don't worry, it's nothing". My first mirage, I thought to myself, an exciting moment in itself. Thinking back to the countless daytime films I watched growing up of thirst-quenched explorers convincing themselves they could see an oasis.

But there it was again! Yes, I was sure I had seen it this time. I sat bolt upright, straining my eyes to see through the hazy shimmers of the summer sun.

"What is it?" Freddie asked, waking from his own daydream.

"There!" I shouted, "There, look!"

And this time, I was sure.

"Camel!" Freddie shouted.

On the horizon slowly emerged the utterly unmistakable form of a sauntering camel. We could make out his back first, rolling from side to side as he took one methodical step after another, then his head nodding with each stride and then each leg emerged from the mist-like haze.

Seeing our first camel was a moment we had long talked about when planning the trip. That was the moment, beyond all other we had decided, that would mark the coming-of-age of the adventure. "If I see just one camel, I'll be happy", I'd often said.

What better represents an adventure in the desert than a wild camel?

We drove up close and pulled over. As I shut my door with a bang, he stopped and slowly swung his head back to look at us. He observed us for a second, then closed his eyes and exhaled through his nose, snorting saliva in all directions as he turned back and restarted his slow, methodical walk. As if to say, "Not another bunch of idiots trying to cross the desert."

I don't know what I was expecting from him. Maybe to jump on his back and take a quick turn about the nearest dune. Maybe a head rub. Even a face full of infamous camel spit would have been better than the look of utter disdain that we got.

We got a quick photo with our prize as he sauntered off into the distance, and we got back on our way.

After a full day's driving, we pulled into the desert and started the camping routine taught to us by our friends in the army many miles ago to avoid being captured by nasty men. It felt a little silly; we hadn't seen anyone for hours.

But, dutifully, we did it anyway. Taking a right turn off the road, we headed south into the desert for around a kilometre, teeth chattering off the vibrations of the harsh, burnt terrain. We then stopped and turned; anyone there? Anyone following us? No one. Nothing. No one for hundreds of miles, let alone following our tracks.

As instructed, we turned on a right angle and headed east for another kilometre to again wait and watch to see if we had any unwelcome guests. We were meant to be doing this at night and with no headlights on. But I would be damned if we were going to miss the sunset.

We found a spot not unlike any other in the desert: hard ground, and a few dry bushes around, but Freddie thought it was the perfect spot for a game of football.

"The hard ground suits my playing style," he claimed.

We stopped and unloaded. Out came the stove and the camp beds — what a godsend they had become. And after a game of football (the hard ground didn't suit Freddie's playing style) and yet another disgusting ration pack (how soldiers could fight on those things is beyond me), we sat back and fell into the sounds of the desert.

It was blissful, nothing but the wind. A rush of joy came over me.

Just look at us, I thought. *Just look at where we are!*

We broke down on the way to our own goddamned leaving party, crashed in a German car park, and pulled Audrey's undercarriage off in Bratislava, but now, against all odds, we were camping out in the Arabian desert. This was adventure, the stuff of dreams and childhood bedtime stories; this was what we were there for.

Although we felt like it, we are not Lawrence of Arabia, we are just two idiots from Oxford, and a retired ambulance from Manchester called Audrey. An unlikely team, but a great team, nonetheless.

The sun ran off into the sand somewhere back towards Istanbul. Sunsets were magical and brief in this part of the world. But then the real show started. The stars came out.

I'm sure you've read many descriptions of the stars in the desert. But my god, it doesn't prepare you for actually seeing it.

It's not really a night's sky at all; there's no blackness to it. The night is almost as bright as day. Every possible spot was taken up by a star shining so brightly you almost needed sunglasses, with only the faintest bit of black sky separating them to remind you what you are looking at.

There is nothing better than lying on your back in the middle of a huge desert and gazing skyward at night. The enormity of it all bends your mind. The sheer number of stars, planets and other things that I've long since forgotten from physics class, all glowing at never seen before brightness. There's no need for a bedside light here.

Stars have always amazed me. You could be looking up at something that happened thousands if not millions of years ago. That light from that star could have been produced when dinosaurs were walking the earth. Yet it was shining on you.

I went to bed blissfully happy. If the journey ended tomorrow, there would be no shame in that. We had made it to places I had never even heard of three months ago. If we flew home tomorrow, it would have all been worth it. Whatever happened now, we were in profit; it was all upside. But what made me even happier was to think that the journey wasn't going to stop tomorrow; we are going to keep going, and we had many more nights like this ahead.

In the morning, the sun arrived bright, and we watched it from our makeshift beds. It crept slowly at first and then, with ever-growing confidence, bound across the desert. It peeked over the horizon, and then when it was sure the coast was clear, jumped out into the open. And before we knew it, it was way up into the sky, casting its golden glow over everything beneath it.

From the point of its first peek over the horizon, we had about twenty minutes to admire it before it started boiling us alive in our sleeping bags. And with our dwindling water reserves, starting the day as a sweaty mess was no way to begin proceedings — it's difficult to come back from that.

Camping in the desert brings a magical silence. None of the usual sounds of this part of the world; no beating goats, no clucking chickens, no call to morning prayer and, most importantly, no spitting. Just the wind as it whistles across the desert, picking up speed with nothing in its way.

We ate our breakfast of porridge laced with chlorine in silence, letting the sun warm us up from the coldness of the night.

We hit a small town early in the drive that day; people rise early here and with a great sense of optimism. It is interesting that we always seem to find the happiest, most optimistic people in the world's most desolate and oppressed places.

Laughing children were being bathed in tin buckets; the local trade sellers quickly stacked watermelons on top of each other, and children rushed off to school under robes that they hope will shield them from the oncoming sun. Gossiping women filled up their first of many large cans of water and started stoking the fires that had been left in ember overnight. The squeak and crack of the first log to be dropped onto the smouldering embers, ready for the first jug of tea and later for shashlik, created the background scent of this land.

Everyone began the day with purpose and joy, whether the

176

local boisterous cockerel or the hungry bleating goat; everyone knew that if you have anything to get done, these three glorious hours between 6 am and 9 am were the hours in which you had relatively humane conditions in which to do it. The air was clear, the sandstorms and thermal shimmies on the horizon were a few hours away, and the country glowed in the warming light of the early morning temperate sun. Past 9 am, forget it, unless you planned to snooze under the shade of an olive tree, you'd be cooked.

In retrospect, perhaps saying their lives were full of joy wasn't the right way to describe the people we saw. Their lives were full of meaning, full of purpose. If you live in a place as desolate as that, where getting through the day and having a meal to eat at the end of it requires real effort, everything you do matters. Fetching the water, bathing your kids, finding food. And I think contentment follows meaningful effort. When everything you want is at the press of a button, it's easy to fall into the trap of doing nothing of consequence. And if you give the mind nothing important to worry about, it will find something to worry about for you.

This theory, however, quickly falls off the rails when you have another life to compare yours to. As we discovered in Eastern Europe, the harsh contrast breeds unhappiness. Thankfully, social media hasn't reached these parts, yet.

Driving through the heat of the day as the mercury rolled over 50, was not the time to be driving an ambulance built to tackle the icy conditions of Manchester's winter. Audrey adapted admirably, only the odd groan and hiss of her radiator to let us know she was struggling. Freddie and I, however, did not.

It was somewhere on that damned road between Turkmenbashi and Ashgabat where we lost our minds. Whether it was the malaria tablets that we were now required to take or the incessant heat, I don't know. But you would not have wanted to come across us in Turkmenistan.

With only three days to cross the country, we spent our days barely speaking to each other, topless, with our shirts wrapped around our faces to protect against the swirling sand with heavy rock playlists screaming out of the van at the highest volume.

The sun, my God, the sun, beat down on us from above, with Audrey's roof only acting as a radiator to pass the heat down onto the two of us, who smelt and looked like only someone could if they hadn't washed for weeks and were in 50-degree-plus heat for the first time.

Without air conditioning, we quickly discovered we had two options in which to cook ourselves. The first was to keep the windows up and allow our bodies to be radiated by the sun coming through the windshield, like being boiled alive in a microwave. The second option was to pull the windows down and to let the 50-degree air outside hit us in the face; more like a fan-forced oven.

The key consideration was whether we wanted to be cooked inside out or outside in. Neither was good.

The key, we found, was in rotation and variety. Just when we thought our organs were at boiling point, we would switch and open the windows to crisp the skin and give our organs a chance to recover. Until our arm hair caught alight, and we had to switch back again, closing the windows and restarting the internal boil. Judging that switching point was a fine and important art to master.

The lack of Audrey's air-conditioning was one thing. However, to compound that, there's no through flow. As any trucker could tell you at great length, as there are no back windows, there was nothing to suck the air through the cabin. The air would just fester around us, growing in humidity. We'd resort to speed and drive as quickly as we could on the dustpan roads, without careening off. In time we realised, even at top speed, it wasn't enough.

Freddie had an idea. We jumped in the back of Audrey, tied everything down as best we could, and then swung open the back doors to encourage some through flow, with one of us tasked to listen intently for any debris, pots, pans, beds, spare fuel canisters, hitchhikers and the like dropping out the back and down onto the road behind us. This slowed us down considerably, as we would have to stop and pick up our belongings and unfortunate hitchhikers as they were scattered across the road behind us, but it was better than being boiled alive.

Eventually, both forms of cooking would get too much, and we'd pull over and dart into the nearest shop that would offer cold relief with yet another bottle of frozen Fanta.

We put our faith in speed, punishing Audrey unmercifully along the dirt tracks, creating dust storms behind, to try and get some sort of air movement through the cabin. We only had one thing on our mind. East, head east. And the sooner we did, the sooner we get out of this damn desert.

I know that we picked up at least two hitchhikers on that stretch — although I can't remember anything about them — God knows what they must have thought of us as they were flung into the rear of Audrey with music blaring and the two of us staring back at them with only the tiny fragments of our face visible between our sunglasses and headscarves. The poor bastards must have regretted their choice of transport immediately.

There is no alcohol in Turkmenistan, probably for the best given our present state of mind. Freddie, I hope he won't mind me saying, has an inclination for the delirious if cooped up for an appropriate amount of time. And no one has such a delirious influence over me as Freddie. The pair of us were as mad as a box of frogs.

We drove on and on, the Rolling Stones at full volume only just heard above the battery of stones kicked up by the wheels that slammed into Audrey's undercarriage. She would lurch from side to side as we crashed through potholes, but she got us through, carrying us onward like wounded soldiers on a stretcher.

Once you've escaped the novelty of the desert, and the illusions of being Lawrence Arabia, you realise how remarkably unre-markable it is. Every mile we edged forward was the same. Each day like the last. Every turn we made was indistinguishable from the last, which made us shout *déjà vu* and swear that we'd driven around in one big circle. We became convinced that we had passed that very bush this morning, seen that dune at least three times today, and how is it 4 pm already?

We were surrounded by life clinging to existence. Every bush, camel and human trying to make do in the most inhospitable environment on earth. Anything further than 100 meters away was clouded in a hazy shimmer, giving us no break from the relentless tedium.

As we continued on, the more sinister side of Turkmenistan

became more and more apparent. Ordinarily, you are only allowed into Turkmenistan with a guide, who has to accompany you 24/7. Any email that we sent home had to be read by a government official first, and our phones could not be used. The whole country is littered with solid gold statues of the president. Even in the poorest areas, there would be colossal gold fountains with the president sitting proudly at the top. Knowing what I now know of how these egotistical shrines were funded from the public purse at the expense of schools and hospitals, it's sickening.

These monuments were clearly designed to garner public support and adulation for the president, or better still, worship? But how could the president develop such a frame of mind? The extraordinary pits of self-confidence you'd have to ascend to before reaching a level at which you'd be able to justify such acts to yourself. If you take power without the backing of the people, you will always be looking over your shoulder.

In spite of all of this, the people of Turkmenistan were friendly and welcoming. They would spot the foreign number plate and force us to pull over to have a picture with them, or just have a chat. The first few times this happened, we thought we were being kidnapped as we were forced off the road, but they just wanted to say hello. It would happen in every town and village we drove through.

There are no strangers in Turkmenistan. The absence of tourism means people take a genuine interest in you, not your wallet. It warmed our hearts and felt like an incredibly fortunate position to be in and a dying fortune in this world at that.

When I asked our new friends about the government, they

would either brush off the subject or give a very generic answer like, "Yes, yes, very good." When we went into the rural areas, they were a little more open to talking. It turned out that every major public area — squares, hotels, restaurants, and the like — was bugged with microphones. One man simply said, "The president is scared about what we have to say, and we are scared of the president." After hearing about the microphones, we would purposely shout "I love Turkmenistan" and "How good is the president?" in public places to sure up our standing.

The whole way through the country, we were treated like royalty, with everyone beeping their horns and shouting as we drove past; it gave us a small glimpse of celebrity life.

We would be invited out to dinner several times each day, with the invitee refusing to budge until we accepted, no matter how many meals we had already eaten. Progress was slow, but our bellies were full, and spirits lifted.

We met one man who had lost his job as a Russian teacher when the president suddenly banned any Russian being taught in schools. He was less reserved with his opinions (he is now an unemployed fisherman) his dream was now to learn English so he could move to England.

Upon meeting us, his eyes lit up, and he embraced me, saying that we could answer his dreams by employing him to teach us Russian back home, we tried to laugh it off, but we could see in his eyes how serious he was.

We sat with him on the banks of a river, his rod extending over the water, motionless.

"One day, I arrived at school, and everything in my classroom had been ripped down, all the books taken. It was like I'd never been there."

Freddie and I stared into the waters, not sure what to say.

"I went to the headmaster, who just said there would be no more Russian lessons and no more me," he welled up as he told his story.

As a small consolation, we gave him our fishing chair and a book to aid his English. He was visibly disappointed, and we were embarrassed that we couldn't do more. How desperate do you have to be to genuinely think two Brits in an ambulance were a viable means of escape and employment? How many other avenues must he have tried and been turned back?

The police, of course, were a hassle. They would pull us over at every checkpoint. But were usually harmless after realising we were from England and would resort to shouting footballers' names at us and then sign their names on the back of Audrey.

Late in the day, we arrived in Ashgabat, the nation's capital. You could see Ashgabat from a long way out. It rises out of the desert like a mirage, a mass of marble glinting in the sun. It's an extraordinary place; every building is coated in marble and lined by palm trees, as if Donald Trump's Manhattan apartment had a love child with Pyongyang. It felt like we had been transported into a completely different world. The city was immaculately laid out and manicured; not a blade of grass was out of place. But no one was around to see it.

There was so much marble, in fact, that Ashgabat holds the record for the highest density of marble anywhere in the world, and they display that fact as you arrive as if it's something to behold.

The opportunity for this remodelling came when the city was completely demolished by an earthquake in 1948 that killed a shocking 110,000 people, close to 10% of the entire population of Turkmenistan. Can you imagine 10% of the UK being wiped out? And I'd never even heard of the disaster until I thumbed my way through our guidebook.

Not to waste an opportunity, the President rebuilt Ashgabat in Trump chic. Huge ministerial buildings replaced homes, and grand avenues led the way to statues of himself gracefully sitting atop a waterfall.

It seems when designing the city, he bought a copy of the Guinness Book of Records and looked for opportunities. Not only does the city boast the highest density of marble in the world, but also the world's largest indoor Ferris wheel (it doesn't work, but that doesn't seem to be important) and the largest fountain in the world (which is actually pretty impressive in a desert, although also incredibly stupid). However, from there, they started running out of ideas, it seems. Next up on their list of world records is the largest mural of a star (I don't think that's a hotly contested category) and the largest image of a Turk carpet (it's not even a carpet, it's just a picture of one). But it's worth pointing out that these are all officially recognised. How did they convince the authorities that a picture of a carpet was a legitimate category? You can just imagine the trembling Guinness Book of World Records assessor.

"But the largest mural of a star isn't an official category, and that's not even a real carpet!"

"Perhaps this envelope will change your perspective on the matter," replying the scary-looking government official.

Upon opening the envelope, his eyes widening "Wow, that's definitely the largest picture of a carpet I've ever seen."

"That's excellent news, now where are you staying? I can recommend some first-class brothels," and that was that, world record complete.

We treated ourselves to a stay in a hotel with an unpronounceable name. Should we have needed it, the hot water didn't work. Oddly, the centrepiece of the hotel was an oil pump, and we were warned not to risk the food by the head waiter. But the rooms were clean(ish), and one of the members of staff tried to be friendly. Also, there was nowhere else to stay.

Once we were settled, we set about looking for all the things we'd been deprived of in the desert, in that most disappointing of western ways, principally beer and pizza. I'm sure Ashgabat has a host of wonderful restaurants serving up the pinnacle of Turkmeni food. But it was grease and carbs that our tummies demanded, and it was that they got.

The only pizza restaurant in town was full of Brad Pitt, and Angelina Jolie look-alikes hiding behind sunglasses and frowns. The pizza was cold and floppy, and the

the waitress made no effort to look impressed when we told her where we had come from.

The next day we left Ashgabat as soon as we could; the emptiness of the place was giving us the creeps. From what we could work out, the only person to live there was the president himself, and we didn't fancy bumping into him.

We headed east back into the desert and its all too familiar heat, dodging the careering lorries as they lurched unpredictably from rut to rut. We came to an unlikely named town, Mary. Like bumping into an old friend in an unfamiliar place, it was a relief to be able to pronounce a town with assurance for the first time in a few weeks.

So named because it was believed by some that Mary (the mother of Jesus — that Mary) was buried here. A town built around an oasis in the desert, it has acted as cooling relief for many a traveller before us. An important stop on the Silk Road, fiercely defended by whoever happened to control it at the time, it's been chucked around for centuries. Even the British fought the Russians here, remarkably less than 100 years ago. A lot has changed since. I pity the poor bastards that had to fight in this heat.

Mary is important today due to its position as the nearest border town to Afghanistan. A wrong turn in these parts, and you could run into sticky situations pretty quickly. Fortunately, Freddie wasn't map reading.

One of the interesting things about Central Asia is that the concept of nation-states is very fluid. People didn't seem to identify too heavily with being Turkmen or Afghani so much as they identify with being Islamic. The border between Turkmenistan and Afghanistan was 50 miles to our south, but that's only because someone in an office in London once said it was.

The borders were just lines in the sand, literally. And as such, an attack on an Islamic land was an attack on them all. And as we neared the border with Afghanistan, upon learning we were English, the locals were very keen to give us their perspective on the war. But it was all done, thankfully, with calmness and humility and followed by several cups of tea. My sort of diplomacy.

I tried to imagine the reverse situation. If the Afghans were raining bombs down on Newcastle and an Afghani walked into a local pub, I wonder if the Geordies would have afforded him the same respect. I suspect not.

Neither Freddie nor I are particularly political, but our sympathies certainly lay with the Afghans on a human level.

As the trip progressed, our armoury of arguments to explain our government's actions in their homeland reduced day by day until only apologies remained.

The day's driving was tough. Our aim was to get as close to the Uzbek border as we could to put us within striking distance of the crossing on the final day of our visa. But the roads were even worse than on our first day.

Freddie had completely lost it by this stage, spending most of his time naked, leaning out of the window, holding out his clothes in the wind to blow the sand out of them. It was a futile attempt.

We were beat and exhausted; trying to cross this stupidly inhospitable country in three days was a huge mistake. And why did we do it? Just because it was there.

Perhaps it would have been prudent to go via Russia, I thought. "Prudent", I heard myself say. *Who the fuck uses a word like prudent? Well, perhaps, it would have been PRUDENT to stay at home this summer and sip beer. But you didn't; you wanted this, now buck the fuck up and enjoy it.*

We pulled over, no further today.

As we wearily stepped out of the van, we were suddenly surrounded by a throng of people. Their sharp, hungry eyes stared at us and, increasingly, at Audrey.

Surrounding the entire van, looking her up and down for a way in, we assumed trouble. Of course, we did, idiots.

It wasn't until the most confident amongst them threw out his hand that we relaxed. "Shalom," he said. What a sweet-sounding word that had become; everyone was friends when it was uttered.

English was in short supply, but they did know "Thank you" and shouted it at us incessantly. But not thank you as we know it but "*I tunk-a you*", said so sweetly and with such a smile that I could start a petition for it to be officially adopted in the Oxford English Dictionary.

The original seems so stale and insincere in comparison. "No, I tunk-a you," we replied with relish.

It turned out we had stumbled upon a late-night swimming session on the banks of the river we had just parked up against.

Relieved, we chucked on our boardies and joined them to wash away the dirt and worries of the day. On returning, feeling refreshed, we realised that we had locked up Audrey with her keys inside. A problem if you're on your way to work in a hurry, a much bigger problem if you're in the middle of the Turkmen desert, two-thousand miles from the nearest Renault dealer. The stresses of the day boiled over as I screamed my frustration into the night.

Our only option was to tear off poor Audrey's sunroof and climb inside. Audrey was now no longer a securely sealed safe room for those long nights in strange places. Anyone could climb aboard and drop in on us whilst we were sleeping. Just another thought to plague my sleep.

Freddie finally finding a playing surface to suit his style

15

Uzbekistan

The next stop on our whirlwind tour of the world's top dicta-torships was Uzbekistan.

The first impression was down the barrel of an AK47 at the border. Regard everything with suspicion until proven otherwise was the unwritten rule of the Uzbek national guard. Especially if it was lurching from pothole to pothole in the form of a British ambulance. I suppose I'd have been suspicious too.

By now, we'd been well schooled to know that the tap of a gun barrel on the car window was code for "get the fuck out and show us your papers." Which we did.

It has a noise like no other, a gun barrel to the windshield. A loud crack, that always comes as a surprise; even when you know it's coming, it sends a shiver straight to your core.

"Batsport!"

We'll add that to the ever-growing list of mispronounced passport requests. Little did it matter; it had its desired effect. We handed them over and were marshalled along.

Like all border guards in these parts, they came in the form of diminishing appearance. The man in charge would be resplendent in full military regalia. His boots polished, his shirt pressed, and his hat stapled into place, covering a manicured and heavily greased barnet. Confident in his requests, pointing you this way and that.

His lieutenant would often make a valiant effort to match his superior but would fall just short. Usually by leaving his hat at home or only polishing one boot.

But from there on down, from rank to rank, clothing would just disappear. The next man in line would wear a beautifully pressed shirt tucked into tracksuit bottoms. His junior wouldn't even bother with the shirt. Finally, we got to the lowest-ranking soldier, who would invariably be wearing a football shirt.

Whether the budget wouldn't stretch to clothe the entire rank or whether they had to pluck new recruits off the football field each morning, I didn't know, but it did have a bizarre look when they stood in file.

Into hut one we strode to start the now accustomed but tedious job of form filling. I can assure you, if you've ever complained about the level of bureaucracy and admin required as part of your end-of-year taxes or monthly work expenses, you have clearly never tried to cross a Central Asian border with a British ambulance. Tedious doesn't begin to describe it.

First, the questions would be about us. First name, second name and then, curiously, full name (you had better not assume that final question was unnecessary and leave it out, oh no). And that's just the start of the seemingly unnecessary questions. Then occupation and salary. Hmmm tricky one. "Student" and "zero" was always met by a raise of the eyebrows. Next came passport details and our visa. Yes, good, we had one. One of the few things we had got right.

Next up were questions about Audrey: age, size, make and model. A rude line of questioning, I thought. I think they were trying to work out if she was going to break down and be left to rust within their borders. Based on her spluttering appearance by this stage, a not unjustified concern.

Once the forms were completed, they were then passed across to a scribe. Who would transcribe them into a book as big as all the Harry Potter volumes stapled together. This book clearly hadn't moved for five years, so what its purpose was, was beyond me. But our answers were recorded at great length, nonetheless.

Now, there were few things more frustrating than watching a man who can't read or write English trying to read and then write English. Particularly if the handwriting he was copying was as bad as mine and especially if he has to write your first name, second name and then your full name, and get confused over the same bits each time.

The Arabic language is all swirls and swooshes; it's all wonderful circular movements of the wrist. So, when they're confronted by a sharp angle in a letter, they panic, a capital "E" brings about a near-total breakdown. The poor man would spot it a couple of words out and start shaking; when they eventually got to that letter, it was a car crash — their brains exploded — they'd never been confronted with something so harsh and ugly in their life. Chuck in the fact that Freddie's second name was Gaelic and mine was double-barrelled, it was pandemonium.

Each word would take five minutes. I'm not criticising; if I had to do the same job in Arabic, it would take me equally as long, if not longer. But when it's 50C outside, you've only got four days to cross this damned country, and a man with the English literacy of a chimpanzee is writing out your name twice, your blood temperature can rise.

I don't know whose name was eventually written in that book, but it certainly wasn't mine or Freddie's.

The second hut, vehicle registration. All the usuals. Original registration documents, tax and insurance, which were calculated, curiously, by the length of the vehicle. And Audrey is long and, particularly unhelpfully, she was made even longer by a sticking-out bit at the end that I think they used to hawk up the stretchers. And, of course, they measured that bit too.

Why did they calculate tax and insurance in this way? No idea. Perhaps the logic was that we took up more space in traffic jams or parking spaces. But we'd long since learned that looking for logic in bureaucratic processes was futile. The one question never to ask a bureaucrat is "why"?

Once this was complete, papers were thrust into our hands, and we were off to the third hut for checking and stamping. Now, as we've already covered, the key thing about someone reading English and then writing it down in English, if they can't read or write English, is that the result is almost certainly not English. Now, if you add to that potent mixture a second man who needed to read and check it, who also can't speak English. What you then have, ladies and gentlemen, is a shit show.

We were sent back to the first hut immediately.

After six hours of this back and forth, we were free and passed into Uzbekistan. I think mostly as a result of the boredom of the guards rather than as a result of any of our documents actually being filled out correctly. But nonetheless, we had crossed the border and lost a day in the process.

At one point in its deep and distant past, Uzbekistan was the centre of the world. Travellers would journey from as far away as Venice in the west and Beijing in the east to marvel at the architectural wonders of its cities, such as Bukhara and Samarkand. It was viewed as the world's capital of culture and intellectualism.

That was then, and this is now. The country's more recent impact on the global consciousness is less impressive.

Like their neighbour Turkmenistan, the Uzbeks have a healthy appetite for records. Listing them all would be as tedious for you as it would be for me, so I'll give you the highlights. For starters, it's the most corrupt country in the world.

That's right; it's not just a little bit corrupt. They added up all the countries in the world on a corruption index, and Uzbekistan rose to the top like a turd in a sewer. What is most impressive about this fact is that when this award was handed out, the local press reprinted the article, with one glaring omission: Uzbekistan's name. They had simply removed their name from the top of the list and shunted everyone else up the ladder and, in doing so, handed the unwanted crown over to Somalia. Really amazing work. You know, if you're competing for something with Somalia, the prize isn't a good one.

However, if you think that is impressive, you haven't heard anything yet. As we crossed the border, to our west stood the country's most recent entry to the Guinness Book of Records. Here, remarkably, they boast the biggest ecological disaster in the world, ever. No destroyed rainforest, no smouldering nuclear reactor, nothing has ever come close to this show of man's ability to destroy nature.

In a crazed desire to keep the Soviet dream alive and to water their cotton fields, the Russians and Uzbeks managed to drain the fourth-largest lake on the planet. And most amazingly, they managed to do it in just twenty years.

The Aral Sea was once comfortably bigger than Lake Michigan; today it's barely a puddle on the ground. It was a huge, nation-sustaining source of fish, commerce, and pleasure. But inch by inch, it receded, each day resigning more boats to a sandy grave.

Apparently, the ships, from family shipping fleets to tourist pleasure cruises, were still out there, the gentle sways of the ocean current replaced by the winds of the desert.

And what compounded matters, when the writing was on the wall of the Aral's demise, the local farmers, in a desperate attempt to keep their crops alive without a water source, started to spray the land with an ever-increasing toxic mix of chemicals. This deadly mix never left this land and haunts it to this day, blowing about in the wind looking for its next victim.

This mad experiment has passed down an unwanted gift to the next generation. Child mortality rate in some of the cities sits at around 30%. The dogged ones that do survive birth have a 38-year average life span to look forward to, tuberculosis accounting for most of their untimely demises.

Not to be outdone by the award for the Most Corrupt Nation on the Planet and the Largest Ecological Disaster in History, there's one further fact worth mentioning. Way out there in its unforgiving desert, Uzbekistan also takes the crown for having the largest chemical weapons plant in the world. Which just so happens to neighbour the largest dump of Anthrax anywhere in the world, abandoned, just waiting for the wind to spread it over the population.

AA Gill, the late Sunday times columnist, once wanted to write a piece on the worst place in the world. They researched for months for the one place beyond all other that offered the lowest opportunities and lowest chance of seeing your 30th birthday. The place they landed on was here, Uzbekistan, presumably in a photo finish with Slough.

In this time of famine in Africa, war in the Middle East, and more natural disasters than you can count on your fingers and toes, the title of the worst place in the world is a competitive trophy. But the Uzbeks won it, hands down.

An introduction to Uzbekistan wouldn't be complete without a quick word on the political situation. When crossing the border from Turkmenistan to Uzbekistan, you really start to shift through the electoral gears as you discover another classic Central Asian democracy.

Here they at least bother to have a vote, which is nice, I guess. The most recent one before we arrived was around eleven years before. Where the president (a loose term in these parts), Islam Karimov, won an impressive 99.6% of the vote. He was such a talented chap, that even the opposition party voted for him. "Suspicious," you say? Well, you'd better not mention that whilst within his borders: the rap sheet of crimes listed against his excellency ranges from simple and relatively innocent slave labour, to torture, to the slightly more serious charge of boiling people alive. So, I'd keep your mouth shut, if I were you.

Our curiosity got the better of us, and every time we spoke to the locals in the streets and in the bars, we asked them about their thoughts on the political system. Amazingly, the majority were either positive about the leader or nonplussed. Whether this was driven by fear, I do not know. But the issue of lack of democracy did not seem a pertinent one to your everyday Uzbek. I guess you can't long for something you've never known.

Or perhaps it's because the politically minded amongst them had already been killed or driven out of the country. The last mass protest against the government ended in the deaths of between 187 and 1,500 Uzbeks, depending on who you believe. It's known as one of the worst political crimes committed in the 21st century. Another Uzbek entry on the global leaderboard of atrocities. But you can see why the politicians are so keen to keep hold of their seats. If you are minded to be loyal to the president, it's pretty cushy work. Parliament only sits twice a year, which gives the president free rein on any decisions that didn't happen to line up with these dates.

You may well ask what the hell we were doing in such a place. Well, to be frank, we learnt most of this after we crossed the border. But the worst place in the world has quite the ring to it, don't you think? It's a very bold claim. A strange nagging curiosity deep inside of you wants to experience it. *Could it really be that bad?* We wondered as we surveyed the landscape stretched out in front of us at the border. We were about to find out.

What we discovered was a completely different side to Uzbekistan from the headlines. This land has been here many centuries before the Soviets, and it's still here in all its charm and mystery, still revealing glimpses of her former glory.

So, we turned our backs on the drained sea, Anthrax dump and the naysayers and headed east, where beckoned an old, glamourous world of mosques, markets and Silk Road trading towns as old as civilisation itself.

We headed north towards Bukhara, and almost immediately,

the harsh climbs of the desert started to recede, and for the first time in a week, we saw greenery, actual plants, a wonderful sight for our dust-addled eyes. Like a cold beer at the end of a long day, the scenery refreshed our minds and souls.

As we drove further and further east, the sand was slowly replaced by gravel and then, little by little, the odd bush and then a tree would appear. Getting greener and greener as we drove.

And then we spotted the source of all this nourishment. Huge canals carved into the landscape, so straight it looked like they had been drawn by God from above.

We pulled over immediately and jumped in. What a relief It was to wash off the sweat, dirt and stress of the border crossing. And as they drained downstream, we felt human again, and our hearts warmed.

As I gazed upwards at the clear blue sky floating on my back, I shouted over to Freddie, who was in a similar pose, "I've got a feeling this place might not be as bad as we feared, you know."

In considerably higher spirits, we found a spot for lunch.

There were only two items on every menu in Central Asia: Shashlik, essentially a kebab on a skewer and Plov, a rice dish with whatever meat they happened to have lying around.

It might sound dull and repetitive only to have two options, but the opposite became true. Upon waking each morning, one of us would turn to the other and announce, "I think it's a Plov day today Freddie!" And both of us would look forward to the first bite from the moment we finished our last at breakfast.

The pair of us became complete connoisseurs on the relative merits of each dish and sat down to lunch as if we were grading an exam rather than eating medieval splodge.

The mere mention of certain cities brings memories of Plov dishes flooding back to this day. Not all positive, it has to be said. In rural Turkmenistan, we found out too late that what we had assumed was sliced chorizo was, actually, sliced horse penis of impressive girth.

Today was a Shashlik day. The restaurant looked like any other in these parts. A smattering of small red plastic chairs, the back of which came up about as high as our knees, were placed around red plastic tables of similar ill proportions. We felt like Gulliver sitting at these restaurants.

The waiter would usually have to be kicked awake or forcibly removed from an intensive game of dice to take our order. Which he would always write down, even though there were only two options.

"*Shashlik pozhaluysta,*" we ordered in our very rusty Russian.

Five minutes later, out would come beautifully barbecued chicken skewers with freshly baked bread. And if we were very lucky, some homemade dip. Heaven. And, drum roll please, for the first time since Georgia, beer. Never has anything tasted so sweet and refreshing. To drive through a desert was intolerable in itself, but to do it without the promise of a cold beer over lunch should be the curse of no man. And all for a cost of about $1 US. If a restaurant only serves two things — they usually do them very well.

We would often sit at these restaurants for hours, watching the world go by, sheltering from the midday sun. Even though we were running to a tight schedule, we were pretty relaxed. Whether we arrive one day or the next didn't really phase us.

At this particular restaurant, as we waited for the sun to die down, a local man in his twenties, with perfect English, approached us. We chatted for a while before he invited us to his house for more food and refreshments around the corner, which we hastily accepted.

The man was clearly well-to-do in the community and shouted at the waiter to bring the bill in a manner that you only learn from being the son of a rich man. He paid our bill, however, so all was forgiven.

His house was opulent in that classic Middle Eastern dictator style: white marble everywhere, matched with gold everything else. At least it was cool.

With a clap above his head, we were served dates and tea. Both delicious.

He then tried to impress upon us how rich, wealthy, and well-connected his family were by showcasing his DVD collection. He was particularly proud of his collection of all three Speed films.

I had other things on my mind and started asking him about the government and the president.

Suddenly he stiffened, and in a clearly rehearsed fashion, barked "Mr Karimov is the best president in the world, a very strong man." Which I thought was an odd way of describing a leader, but perhaps revealing.

Wanting more than the rehearsed speech, I asked him about the killings, which flustered him. The poor man just wanted to show off his DVD collection.

Years of brainwashing hadn't quite prepared him enough. His family had clearly benefited from the regime, not the man to get any truth out of.

Looking back, it was incredibly reckless of us to poke him in this way. The way the government has treated ordinary Uzbeks was, of course, terrible. But what did we expect to gain from such questions? Did we really think he would suddenly change his mind and then go on a crusade of redemption? More likely, his well-connected father would have made our lives incredibly difficult with one phone call to a bored policeman. We were driven by an anger, a sense of wanting justice, that didn't really make sense given we'd just arrived in the country and had little knowledge of the intricacies at play or met any of the victims. Perhaps we were still remorseful of how little we could help the fisherman in Turkmenistan. I think, however, more likely, we were driven by a Western arrogance that "our way is better; let me show you." That same arrogance, from people in higher places than us, has done more to contribute to the current state of this country than anything else. We made our excuses and left. Bukhara was awaiting us.

Bukhara was one of the cities we dreamed of when leaving England. The city is as old as the dawn of time. Educated men and women in white Land Cruisers have poked and prodded its sands and concluded that people have lived here for at least five millennia and the early structures of the city that rose out of the sand in front of us now, is likely at least half that age. And you can sense it when you arrive. We felt like Silk Road traders striding into an oasis after months in the desert. The chance of a shower, a cup of tea and perhaps even another beer put sparks in our eyes and extra weight on the accelerator.

Like anywhere, the city has now overgrown its ancient, fortified walls into rolling suburbs, but the core, the beating heart of the city, is still there, as it has been for centuries. As we crossed into the old town and walked under the walls that have defended this bastion of culture from everyone from Stalin's Red Army to Genghis Khan and every despot dictator in between, we could still sense the importance of the place. It's the energy. In its centre, it's still dense, buildings compacted and squeezed together over centuries, in the way you imagine such historic places to be, with overladen merchants pulling their wares down the road on outstretched carts bouncing from pothole to pothole, offering little warning before they crash into your thighs.

We walked the thronging markets that surround the oasis; you can buy anything from a pistol to a stuffed sparrow, if you so wish, with as many spices and aromatics for a bible-basher to believe he's one of the wise men himself. And even the odd yard of silk, ensuring that this historic trading place stays in touch with its roots as one of the nervous centres of the Silk Road.

In the winding streets, not built for the width of a car, we played a constant game of chicken with horse carts, lorries, motorbikes, donkeys, blacked-out land cruisers and pissed-off camels. The towering walls on either side surrounded us and amplified the sound of beeping horns, revving engines and spitting camels. Ironically, the only form of transport that gave any warning of their proximity were the ones that bore the least risk of injury. Brightly decorated bicycles came with customised bells (if you could call them that), serenading us with everything from The Beatles to *Happy Birthday* before they smashed into our shins.

The crowds were thick, but the old silk traders resting on their way between China and Venice and back again had largely been replaced by weekending Uzbeks and Muslims making pilgrimages from further afield. Handsome people, chiselled, probably more by the incessant summers and harsh winters than by breeding. Most with absorbing deep green and blue eyes that look through you to your souls.

The late afternoon is the best time to wander the streets. The setting sun filtered by the desert sand that was permanently suspended in the air, which created a golden hue on everything. And it just so happens that this golden hue reflected onto some of the most magnificent architecture in the world. Every shade of brilliant blue you can imagine tilled over the buildings with the turquoise minarets reflected in the many sculpted pools of water. It was impossible to be in a bad mood.

The Islamist architectural footprint on the world is remarkable. Give me a mosque in all its imperial blues and huge domes over a European cathedral, any day. The colours are so romantic. The grey of European stone replaced by tiles of midnight
blues and turquoise. These colossal structures, built out of the sand in the scorching heat, are awe-inspiring.

When the authorities recently tried to repair the facade of these great mosques, they couldn't for the life of them figure out how to replicate the brilliant blue of the tiles. Everything that they tried wasn't quite brilliant enough, or would wear quickly. Until, by chance, they discovered the blue paint was mixed with human blood to give it its unique colour and durability. Looking around, I can tell you it would have taken a lot of blood to coat this city. And it's seen its fair share of wars to top up its supply. Armies throughout history have emerged from the shimmers of the desert. The Mongols started it; Ghengis Khan besieged Bukhara for 22 days in the 12th century before killing everyone in the citadel and enslaving the rest. And the Russians picked up where they left off. The city feeling the pounding wrath of the Red Army in more recent times.

But the city lives on. Life here hasn't changed much for thousands of years, not the stuff that matters. There might be the odd phone or TV screen, but the important things in life remain unchanged.

The men sit about for hours in the afternoon shade playing games of dice, every now and again leaning back in their chairs and roaring with laughter with their hands holding tight over their shaking bellies. The women sit about chatting and giggling, with the kids running around laughing and jumping in the pools of refreshing water.

You could close your eyes and imagine you were in any century you picked.

We sat and watched. There was something that felt out of place to me. Something that wasn't quite right. After a while, I managed to put my finger on it. The men, women and children sat in front of me were comfortably the happiest people I have ever seen. We arrived with dire warnings labelling Uzbekistan as the worst place in the world, with more ecological disasters and political massacres than you could count. But here, in this grand old city, the people were not only happy, but ecstatic. I could not imagine a more idyllic scene. When you live in such places, and it's clear that you are just a grain in the sands of time, what's the point in rushing?

Offer any of them a job in an air-conditioned office in London with harsh neon lights and strict 8 am to 6 pm working hours, and I think the reaction it would solicit would quickly tell you who actually has the better quality of life in this world.

The resilience and positivity of the people had completely won me over. I chastised myself for arriving there with such prejudices. Someone has since said to me that they hate all governments and love all people. I think that's about right.

The next day we rose early to beat the heat and walked between each remarkable mosque visiting medieval bazaars en route with hawkers selling everything you can imagine. And then to the Ark of Bukhara, a fantastic fortress that's built in the style of a 5-year-old's beach sandcastle with sand-coloured and perfectly rounded walls. This is where the soldiers of Genghis Khan were housed following their takeover, which sent my imagination into overdrive. We returned to the shade of the central square to sit around the centrepiece of the entire city, a stunning oasis known as Lyab-i Hauz. Flanked by three of the most impressive Mosques in the city on each side, this architectural ensemble has barely been touched since it was built in the 16th century.

We laid about the oasis, basking in its cool relief, drinking copious amounts of tea until the sun finally started to drop and let us emerge from our hiding spot. It was one of the highlights of the entire journey.

To look at the local people of Bukhara was like looking at people from another century. The man sitting next to us in the cafe, grinning through his weather-beaten face, could easily have been a cavalryman from Alexander the Great's army. The man walking his camel, head down with a wide hat to protect him from the heat, could easily have been a fabled trader of the silk road stopping off for a much-needed break on his journey from Venice to Beijing. The camel, incidentally, was dressed even better with a glorious Turkish red rug across his back as he looked down his nose at us. He knew how good he looked.

Their faces haven't changed, and neither has their fashion sense. Silk was still a big deal here; the longer the silk robe, the better it seemed. Some gentlemen, who looked particularly pleased with themselves, sported silk robes that trailed behind them in the dust.

We lost ourselves in the romance of it all; this was the land of the Great Game. Back when England and Russia were the foremost world powers and had the associated level of paranoia over who was going to steal whose toys.

That period of history inspired an unknown number of books and poems, most of which bored us to sleep in our English classes when we were younger, and it was all played out here, beneath our feet. This was frontier country, with every drop of the romance that comes with it. The border posts were now no longer manned by people with names like Smith and Williams, defending the Empire, but replaced instead with hardnosed policemen with long memories.

Uzbekistan suffers from chronic deflation. So much so that they have huge electronic signs on the side of the road showing the official exchange rate to the US Dollar. Each day it would get higher and higher. So, make sure you pay for your hotel room on arrival, otherwise, the cost can double by the time you check out.

We quickly realised that it would take too long to count the cash, so we would "estimate". A handful of cash was about $10, a bag of cash around $50 and two bags roughly $100.

When paying for a hotel room, one bag of cash usually did the trick. And if we got a bemused look from the front desk, we would continue to hand over fistfuls of cash until his frown subdued.

We were either grossly overpaying for everything, or we had stumbled upon standard practice, as the reaction from storekeepers across this land were, on the whole, accepting.

But this threw up a bookkeeping complication. Knowing how much money we had on us at any one time was damn near impossible.

We would keep track of the number of bags of cash we would have — but we could often be out by a few hundred dollars each way. Which, in a country where the average meal costs $1, is a lot of money to misplace.

We found this out the hard way, four hours out of Bukhara at a petrol station. By the time Freddie made the dreadful discovery that one of the bags of "cash" actually contained our sleeping bags, we had filled up all three of Audrey's main and spare tanks, as well as filling ourselves up on lunch at the neighbouring restaurant.

Explaining this to the owner of the establishment proved tricky. He got quite excitable, assuming, wrongly, that this was all part of our game and our intention all along.

He insisted that we drive to the nearest bank to withdraw cash. Which was back in Bukhara, an eight-hour round trip.

Realising there was no other option, we reluctantly agreed. But as we jumped back into Audrey, he shouted that he needed some sort of guarantee that we would return. He wanted a deposit.

He was clearly not in the mood to trust these poorly bearded Westerners — quite right.

We offered up Freddie's QPR scarf, which was met with bafflement. QPR clearly represents little value outside of West London.

"No," he said, "him," and pointed to Freddie.

Freddie's face dropped. I shrugged.

"Come on, mate; you can't leave me here with this man,"

Freddie said.

I made a lame attempt to demonstrate with the man. But secretly, I thought spending a few hours apart for the first time in months was exactly what we both needed. Even if it wasn't in the safest of circumstances. But I pushed that to the back of my mind.

"We've got no other option, I'm afraid, mate. Out you get."

"He looks like a nice enough guy," I said, trying and probably failing to seem confident in my character judgement. He looked like the type of guy who would slice you apart with a curved dagger the moment you turned your back.

Freddie finally consented. Good man. A real team player.

And just like that, I was steaming back towards Bukhara, windows down, Rolling Stones blaring at high volume and alone for the first time in months.

If only.

Our increasingly agitated new creditor was apparently not convinced that leaving Freddie as a deposit was sufficient to ensure I would return. So his brother, Ali, was instructed to come along for the ride. I'm not sure who was more pissed off about this, me or Ali. But Ali certainly didn't make any effort to hide his displeasure.

And that was that. Freddie was left to help man the pumps for bemused Uzbekis, and I was destined to an eight-hour road trip with Ali, who looked no more trustworthy than his indebted brother.

I wasn't sure who I'd rather be. If Freddie went missing, at least I could alert the authorities of his approximate whereabouts. If I didn't return, I could be anywhere from here to Baghdad before the sun rose.

I tried my best to make conversation in my usual way, listing the names of footballers. But whatever rapport I had with this poor man quickly disappeared when I immediately took three wrong turns and caused an almighty traffic jam by driving the wrong way down a one-way street.

After eight hours of getting lost and pissing off my new mate, I returned to find Freddie, thankfully still at the pumps. He was relieved to see me and full of stories of sheep filled hatchbacks. Freddie, despite his misgivings, had enjoyed himself. Somehow, chatting away with the fuel attendants.

He was given a place to lie and watermelon to eat. Every new arrival at the pumps was told the story of how Freddie came to be there, including his attempt of bartering with a QPR scarf, which every time was met with hysterics.

"Including a guy," as Freddie would explain, "who didn't have much of a leg to stand on as he turned up in his Lada with what appeared to be five sheep on the back seat and on leaving, he had to push start the car himself!"

But despite the comical respite, ever since leaving Bukhara, my nerves had been rising. It was here that we were told to be especially vigilant by Corporal Fisher back at the army barracks. And to add to that, the British Foreign Embassy had warned us against all but essential travel to this part of Uzbekistan, citing that "border areas could be land mined and terrorist attacks can't be ruled out." But it was our only route through. It was an important part of our puzzle linking us to Kazakhstan and on to Russia.

The cause of these forewarnings and my sleepless nights was directly south of here, the border with Afghanistan. You could drive straight there if you took a right-hand turn in the next village. But you shouldn't do that; it's Taliban country.

When the Taliban first took the border town, they killed everything that moved: men, women and children, livestock. Nothing escaped their fire. It was one of the first areas to be invaded by the US after 9/11 and perhaps unsurprisingly, the border that we were now driving along was now the second most fortified in the world, after the South Korean / North Korean border. The Uzbeks didn't want Tashkent to be this decade's Kabul, understandably.

As we drove, my eyes flickered from left to right, and my imagination ran wild. Every parked car or pile of rubbish became the hiding place of a Taliban ambush. I watched intently as a Land Cruiser grew larger in my wing mirror, coming at us at speed; the driver swerved into the other lane to overtake, the blacked-out passenger window slid open as he drew level, and a man in sunglasses and a headscarf stared at me from a matter of meters away. A smile cracked across his face, and the driver sped off. I sat back into my seat, relieved.

As we drove within spitting distance of the border, we couldn't help but think of the people caught up in these horrible wars, and I took it upon myself to do a little research. Shockingly Afghanistan has lost fifty per cent more people in the war than the US lost in the entirety of the Second World War, from a population roughly the size of California. And all for reasons that I couldn't recall at the time.

However, despite all of this and, contrary to the many warnings we got (mostly from people unqualified to give them), we encountered nothing but hospitality. Driving through any town would take several hours as the locals spotted the foreign number plate, flagged us down, greeted us enthusiastically and offered us anything from a pomegranate to a bed for the night in order to make our stay a memorable one. Every now and again, the war would be brought up, and an attempt would be made to explain our government's terrible misdeeds and ignorance. But although we could see the anger and pain in their eyes, the people we met were always incredibly polite and respectful, and we never felt this anger was going to blow over into a desire for revenge. By the end of each conversation, we usually completely sympathised with their view, and these conversations sowed the seeds for what is likely to be an everlasting distrust in what our government and media tell us. The lines between good and evil blur when you look them in the eye.

My calm and reasonable mind would set with the sun, however. Night-time, sleeping out in the desert, was a different story. The darkness brought no barriers to my thoughts, and soon my body was stiff with terror. Any distant crunch was the Taliban creeping up on us, any snap was a snake crawling its way up the leg of my camp bed.

Freddie had told me a few days prior that snakes could sense warmth for miles, like a shark can taste blood. The thought of waking up with a serpent cuddling me in my sleeping bag hadn't left me since, and sleep became rare.

Morning always brought perspective. As the sun came up, I could see again that there was nothing for miles, barely even a scrub or a tree and certainly no terrorists, or snakes for that matter. But it didn't make up for my lack of sleep, and I knew that at the next sunset, the barriers to my worries would be lifted once more.

The worst places were the checkpoints. And with the risk of terrorism as it was, there were a lot of checkpoints. As Audrey slowed as we approached, my heart thumped through my chest. These checkpoints were magnets for news headlines. The men that guarded them experienced a cocktail of emotions, from complete boredom for days on end to moments of paralysing fear. Nobody blinked at another news bulletin announcing an incident at a checkpoint, no twenty-one gun salute, no tales of bravery or life immortalised in a war memorial, just your name added to the stats. This was not what these young guys joined the army for.

And you could see it in their eyes. Suspicion as we approached quickly turned to empty-eyed boredom as they realised we were not a threat, as they pressed their face against our window. But they still had to complete their checklists. And for that, we had to wait. These checkpoints took on a different tone to their Turkmen cousins; they seemed more serious, they had more intensity in their eyes and fidget in their trigger fingers.

The issue, we learnt, was that Uzbekistan has a very fluid border with Afghanistan where all sorts of nasty people came and went as they pleased. They even have a homegrown branch of Al Qaeda called the Islamist Movement of Uzbekistan, or IMU for short. The good-natured terrorists had gone as far as to save Western journalists a few seconds on each story by choosing an acronym-friendly name.

The Uzbeks are trying to get on good terms with the Western world, so they didn't particularly want to be seen as a country that accommodated terrorists. So, they arm their trigger-happy border guards and policemen to the teeth to try and rid themselves of these folk. Unfortunately, a moral conscience didn't appear chief among the recruitment requirements.

At one checkpoint, we were pulled out and told to stand in

front of Audrey, facing a line of men holding AK47s. Now, I admittedly don't know a lot about guns, but gun safety didn't seem to be a huge concern. The lower-ranking men threw them around with wild abandon. They leant on them; they poked things with them, they dropped them. And, just like a falling iPhone that always lands screen down, a falling AK47 seems to always land muzzle pointing at me. Any number of loose stones could dislodge that trigger, but they didn't seem to care as they continuously threw their weapons off their shoulder and looked surprised when I jumped up and screamed, trying, in my mind, to avoid a flying bullet.

Freddie found the whole thing hilarious.

"You wouldn't laugh so much if it landed pointing in your direction!" I shouted.

"I know; that's why I make sure I laugh when it lands facing you!"

Now, it would not have been fair to say that all the police and border guards in Uzbekistan were this way, but neither would it be wise to hang around to find out. These men had every power to make our trip to their corner of the earth a misery, so we made every effort to appease them and move on as quickly as possible.

On one occasion that we were pulled over, we asked why to the one half-English speaking cop; he replied that we were coming from an area known to be populated by terrorists and other delinquents and seeing an ambulance with a British number plate driven by two men clothed only in boxer shorts and shirts wrapped around their heads had caused some alarm amongst his men. On some level, I could see his point.

Fortunately, we were waived through without too much delay. But the jittery look in the eye of one of the soldiers didn't entirely convince me he was in control of his emotions, which unnerved me slightly. *Perhaps we should start taking this a little more seriously*, I thought. I suggested to Freddie that we should sharpen up a bit.

At the next river we came across, we washed, bathed and shaved. Freddie took it one step further and revealed an Ascot racecourse tie from the back of the van from our very brief stint working there. What his original plans were for this tie was beyond me.

"This should do the trick," he exclaimed proudly as he tied it up loosely around his neck, looking in the wing mirror for assistance.

It didn't seem to dawn on him that wearing a tie without a shirt would probably only worsen our image in the eyes of the local constabulary — but on we went nonetheless, with Freddie looking particularly pleased with his new accessory.

There are two sides of every coin, of course. The more adolescent fingers on the triggers of AK47s, the fewer tourists. This was a beautiful thing. When in the south of France, you would have to jostle for a spot on the beach and wait for hours for a seat in a restaurant, no reservations of any kind were required in Uzbekistan. The restaurants were mostly empty, and the hotels certainly were. And that's before we get onto the traffic, which was non-existent.

Slowly, we learned how to approach the checkpoints. Now each time we were pulled over and shoved into the policeman's hut, we remained absolutely calm and detached. It was amazing the effect this had disarming the initial hostility of the police. The key, we learned, was just to wait it out, whether that took one hour or five. The first hour would be spent with our captors shouting in our faces and demanding money for X, Y, and Z infringement and us remaining silent. In the second hour, they would give up, and we would all sit in silence. In the third hour, friendly chit-chat would start, and then in the fourth and fifth, we'd all be best friends passing around cups of tea and nuts until they got bored of us and told us to move on.

It was just a waiting game, and as we had all the time in the world, we held all the cards.

Suddenly we were no longer approaching the checkpoints with nerves, but almost relief. A few hours out of the oven that was Audrey and into a shaded police hut with a never-ending supply of tea was exactly what the doctor ordered. If the checkpoint appeared around lunchtime and our tummies were beginning to rumble, we'd deliberately be awkward to ensure those hours of shade and tea would be ours.

On we drove north, searching for Tashkent and, with it, the welcome border with Kazakhstan, signalling, in our mind, relative safety. The closer we got, the more I relaxed. We let ourselves go back to restaurants and chat with the locals. We were out of the danger zone now and returning to civilization; the capital was within a day's drive. That night would be our last night in the desert; the next day, we'd be having a warm shower in a bland Tashkent hotel. Surrounded by four walls, a roof, and, most importantly, a locked door.

Happy with our work for the day, we pulled into a local restaurant for a plov and beer. We found a merry atmosphere with the other tables full of locals ready to drain their

drinks and dance. We flipped a coin for who would drive to

the campsite, Freddie won and promptly got stuck in. I sat back and enjoyed the show. When I finally managed to drag Freddie away from the festivities after many "one last beer" I was tired and ready for my bed.

"Screw it. Let's sleep on the side of the road tonight. I don't have the energy for the rigmarole of our army routine." We pulled up and made camp in a field neighbouring a farm. As we arrived, the farmer came out and gave us a warm welcome with some of his apples. I tried to show some gratitude through my tiredness.

I collapsed into bed. Sleep, however, was brief. I stirred with the sense of presence nearby and pressure on my neck. I tried to ignore it and return to my much-needed sleep. But the pressure on my neck got harder. I opened my eyes to see gold teeth glistening in the moonlight inches from my face, his hand around my neck. I can remember the force of his grasp around my throat to this day. I gasped for air as the grip tightened: firm and then loose, and then firm again.

I sharply inhaled and tried to sit up, throwing an arm out to Freddie next to me. But the force of the man's grip wouldn't allow me to. His eyes were narrow and looked straight through mine.

I had come face to face with my greatest fear, but the panic and irrationality of my imagination didn't stir; my mind was sharp and clear. The two men with their hands on our throats were dressed in headscarves and robes and were flanked by two more men. I could only see the eyes of my captor, which were fierce and blue; the rest of his face was shrouded in a black and white headscarf. His arms flexed as he pressed down on my throat once more. He looked in his early twenties, about my age, but it was hard to tell.

For a while, nothing was said. I couldn't speak. The only noise was of heavy breathing, from both sides. Neither knowing what to do.

I looked again into the eyes of my captive, and all I could see was fear. His eyes darted shiftily from left to right waiting for one of his mates to do or say something. Anything.

Now that they had us, they didn't know what to do with us.

My mind went into overdrive, days of reading about the Taliban brought me to worrying conclusions. Who were they, and what did they want from us? Were they the Taliban or were they just local youths looking to escape the tedium?

He released his grip allowing me to sit up and properly look at them. Now my eyes had adjusted to the light; he didn't look a day older than 16. It looked like he hadn't washed or slept for weeks. His eyes kept darting back to the others, waiting for instructions.

Then the anger took hold, and the screaming started. Fingers pointed in our faces, and saliva moistened our clothes. Their voices fired with passion like they were unloading years of pain and frustration. All in Arabic. All completely incomprehensible.

Freddie and I stared at them, unable to reply. After a while, the shouting turned inward. The more passionate members of the group arguing with the more hesitant.

They were clearly trying to work out what to do with us. Their pre-planning hadn't got this far. The more passionate amongst them, who seemed to be winning the argument, didn't seem to have our best interests at heart.

Just as they had appeared to reach a consensus and walk back towards us our friendly farmer rushed onto the scene, clearly awoken by the commotion. This flustered the junior members of the team. With the presence of a witness, this had suddenly all got quite real. They fled.

The remaining two members lurched for us, arms outstretched, but the farmer blocked their path. We jumped to our feet. We now outnumbered them, three to two. They paused for a moment and then turned on their heels and followed the others into the darkness.

Relieved and exhausted, we collapsed onto our beds. I rolled onto my back, staring up into the sky, clutching my throat and breathing heavily. What had just happened? The farmer shouted "IMU" into the night's sky and thrust up his hands in disgust. But those young men didn't seem like the ones from my nightmares. It wasn't evil in their eyes; it was anger and pain.

God knows what would have happened if the farmer hadn't arrived at that exact moment. At the time, I couldn't work out whether it meant something or not, I still can't. To this day, I don't know if that was a harmless run-in with a group of drunken youths looking for a fight or one of the greatest and luckiest escapes of our lives. I don't think we will ever know.

It could have been five minutes before I regained composure. I turned to Freddie, who was staring ahead. Panic then finally took hold.

"We need to get out of here, now," I shouted to Freddie.

We ran and ran hard. We jumped in Audrey, not really taking time to pick up our things, and drove. We kept driving and driving until the sun broke — it was only then that we felt safe enough to go back to sleep and, even then, in the front cab with the doors locked.

* * *

Tashkent, the capital of Uzbekistan, is a city like any other city really. Full of people trying to make do.

If you ever come here, for God's sake, do not drink the water, it turned my insides into molten lava, and I hope the only positive thing that arose from that damned experience was that you've learned my lesson.

At first glance, the city lacks charm. On your second and third glance, you'll be reminded to trust your first impression. We vowed to get in and get out pretty quickly.

The city itself was corroded by the many years of Soviet occupation more than most. Huge brutalist apartment buildings are the scars that remain.

Today market traders hawk Chinese air conditioners, Korean microwaves, and Taiwanese televisions. Their younger apprentices sell the more fashionable knock-off Russian watches and fake DVDs. Men squatting on the side of the street suck hard on failing cigarettes, whilst watching you with empty expressions.

As our journey continued, the tide was slowly turning from Arabic charm to Russian crass and aggression; you could feel the Russian influence in Tashkent, and I didn't like it. Whatever was there before the Soviets took over, it was there no longer.

It had always been our plan at some point in the journey, if we made it so far, to shred our Western clothes in favour of something cooler and more befitting our surroundings. And it was in Tashkent where we finally got around to this task. We hit the market stalls, where everything and anything was sold. A place of complete madness. A competition of who can shout the loudest to sell their frock that was the same price and looked no different to his neighbour in the next stall. When your goods look no different to your neighbour's, business was won by yelling. The strategy of differentiation was yet to hit these parts.

We were in the market for a good robe, and this was where you came for such things. Thousands of them, in all different colours and sizes, hoisted up on elaborate pulley systems. All it took was an accidental meeting of the eye with a market trader for him to point at us, shouting, "Yes, yes, yes!" his other hand bringing the nearest item of clothing and throwing it on our backs: "You like?"

"Errrrm, not exactly my style," I said, referring to a leather jacket of such fakery that you could shave in its reflective qualities. Not to mention it was 40C out and not the weather for such garments.

We pointed to the robes.

"Ahhh yes, verrrry good choice," he said with an elongated "very" to really hammer the point home.

Before I could blink, the robe was thrown over my head, and I was marched to the nearest mirror.

I'm not sure what you look for when trying on Arabic robes, but this one seemed to strike the right tone. The price was haggled over, and a deal was struck. The time elapsed from walking into the booth to coming out looking resplendent in our new Arabic robes? About two minutes flat. My kind of shopping.

Before we came to this part of the world, we heard a lot of nonsense about haggling, and like all the nonsense you hear about Central Asia, it's largely true.

The initial price the man quoted us would have made even the most hardened of Harrod's store clerks blush. Whether he was chancing his arm on an ignorant tourist, or he kicked off with that price with everyone, I do not know. However, our ignorance had long since passed, or so I thought. I fake laughed and quoted a price around 10% of the initial offer. At this point, the man suddenly lost all ability to speak English. A profitable tactic, I'm sure, but we were wise to it. We turned on our heels and left. He let us take two steps and then shouted back at us in his rediscovered English.

"Okay, Okay, okay — we meet in the middle."

"No." We responded, turning back out of the shop.

"Okay, okay, okay. Just take it; I won't look; I'll do it just for you, my friend," he said, mock shielding his eyes as he did.

He picked up the robe, had it in a bag, and printed the receipt in one fell swoop.

Happy with our morning's work, it was time for tea. Walking to the cafe, we realised that our new robes were made of nylon, and the simple act of walking created enough static to start a bush fire.

At our hotel, remarkably, we met a fellow European in the lobby. Her name was Rachelle, she was from Switzerland, and she didn't like us very much. I think she got a hit from wowing everyone back home with her two-week trip to Uzbekistan, so to meet two idiots that were attempting something far more audacious ruined her self-proposed social standing somewhat. She declined our dinner invitations.

Freddie, who hadn't met another woman who could speak more than a few words of English to him in over a month, was more than a little disappointed. He would have to put up with my company and conversation for yet another evening.

In these more distant parts we began to meet people on similar journeys and it was during such meetings that we were introduced to the strange world of overlanding. Overlanding is a sport of sorts where hardy travellers drive, bike or walk the longest possible distances on earth. It just so happened that our route, London to Beijing, was one of the over-landing 'holy grails'. Along with London to Cape Town and Anchorage in Alaska to Santiago in Chile. Sat in youth hostels and bars, we could spot these men, and they would always be men, from a mile off. They would dress like Victorian explorers in off-cream shirts and trousers and tie handkerchiefs around their necks with big broad-brimmed hats. It was quickly apparent that we had nothing in common with these types. You'd see them approach, and you just know they're going to ask you about equipment, and there's little I care for less.

"Which sat phone do you have?" they would ask, whilst holding theirs proudly, just waiting for an opportunity to show off its features.

"We don't."

"What do you mean you don't? How do you call when you're in the desert?" he scoffed in reply.

"We don't," I was intentionally rude, trying to make it clear I had no interest in his line of questioning.

They would look at me hard through narrowed eyes to see if I was joking.

"Bloody hell, are you trying to contact the aliens with that thing?" said Freddie, returning from the bathroom mid-conversation.

"Er, no," they would say, incredulously. "It's incredibly

important to have one." They would stand up and look down their noses at us in an attempt to regain their pride. "Do you have a phone at all?"

"Yep, we have a Nokia 3210," which was met by silence. "It has snake on it", I clarified.

They never laughed.

These men had spent years preparing for their trips, and they found our casualness insulting. As if we'd turned up to their wedding in boardies and flip-flops.

Happy with our administrative work in Tashkent, the next day we made a break for the border with Kazakhstan. It was the last day on our visa, so we rose early to give us a day to cross the border. Which was when the troubles started.

Audrey, of course, wouldn't start. The key went into the ignition only to be followed by that dreaded click, click, click.

"For god's sake, Audrey, start! Please start!"

"It's too hot to wrestle with you now."

I slumped over the wheel in a resigned heap, already sweating heavily. It was only 9 am.

I pulled myself up and went around and opened the bonnet, not really knowing what to look for. I instructed Freddie to pump the accelerator. As he did so, hot diesel squirted out all over me. Drenched in hot, foul-smelling and highly flammable liquid was not how I had envisioned this day starting.

Inspecting the area from where the diesel squirted, I found the fuel filter, a piece of wire mesh designed to filter out bits and pieces that weren't meant to be in there, was caked in sand. The two days of no driving whilst we were in Tashkent had allowed all the sand that we had collected from the deserts of Central Asia to solidify and stop any fuel passing through to the engine.

Fortunately, this was one issue we had prepared for. The fuel filter was replaced, I changed my clothes, and we were good to go.

Feeling pretty proud of how far our mechanical skills had advanced in such a short time, we headed to the border.

On the drive to the border, having had a few days to process, my thoughts turned back to our captors. My emotions had turned from anger and hatred to empathy.

The mere mention of Al Qaeda, if that's what indeed they were, conjures up all sorts of nasty thoughts, from filmed beheadings to banning girls from attending schools. And I'm not doubting that the hierarchy was clearly made up of sick and evil men. But the foot soldiers, the men that we met, what if they were just displaced adolescents offered a better life?

Put yourself in their shoes; imagine if your village had just been bombed by an unmanned American drone — for no obvious reason. And then the Al Qaeda came through and offered you a job and revenge. Thinking back to the bundle of anger and emotions I was when I was 16, I would have signed up in a heartbeat.

If you had the choice between walking around with an AK47 and sleeping in the mountains, or driving sheep for the rest of your life, what would you choose?

We're all exactly alike. We all have cultural tendencies that bewilder others, of course we do; the British play cricket, the American's put maple syrup on bacon — I've seen them do it. But when you cast aside these irrelevant differences that nasty men like to point at, we're all the same.

With that understanding, it seemed that the policies of Western governments and their inability to safeguard civilian lives in these parts was so hopelessly misguided. If only they spent some time out there before raining down bombs from 20,000 feet.

Before arriving in Uzbekistan, of all the places we have travelled, we had never had such dark warnings. And they were right. We experienced the subject of these warnings directly. Their dark protestations, very nearly, came true. The country was beset by political atrocities, and terrorists roam freely. So why did I feel so overwhelmingly positive about it? Why had I come to love the infectious laughter of its people, the golden final light of each day reflecting on its ancient architecture, and the wonderful slow pace of life? I've come to realise that it's not one of the most intoxicating and uplifting countries despite these troubles, but because of them. The harsh contrast of life here makes it more vivid.

This fact is lost, of course, on the armchair travellers; the cynics, the huffers and puffers of middle England, always feeling empowered to dish out dire premonitions to those with more imagination and bravery. I've come to think we lead such boring lives these days that we tell ourselves myths of safety and security to justify our lack of adventure.

Stupidly we listened to these people. And as soon as we crossed the border, we braced for the worse, constantly imagining everything that could go wrong. But the constant smiles on the faces of the locals belied all of that and quickly won us over, even with our brief stint as a captive. The ever-growing number of ear-to-ear grins started to nag at our prejudices and then melted them away in a torrent. The constant hospitality, particularly from those without much to give, was truly heartwarming.

It taught me a lifelong lesson never to listen to cynics. If you expect people to be mean, dispirited and downright rude, they, on the whole, will be.

A traveller in a foreign land meets a stranger travelling in the opposite direction. "Excuse me," the traveller says. "What are the people like in the town ahead of me?" The stranger replies with another question "What were they like in the town you've just left?"

"They were kind, hospitable, generous and wise."

"Well, I expect that's what you'll find they're like in the next town," says the stranger.

* * *

We arrived at the border crossing illustrated on our map, and it was chaos. Donkeys, chickens, horses and children roamed everywhere, with exasperated border guards trying and failing to provide some sort of order and security to proceedings.

We parked up and were immediately shouted at by one such security guard who had clearly decided we were an easier target than the three-year-old crossing the border unaccompanied behind him.

The subject of his tirade quickly became clear. This border crossing was only for horses, donkeys and pedestrians. "Neit Tourists!" He shouted. Who has a border crossing for donkeys in this day and age? The Kazakhstanis do.

226

But no matter, if we wanted to cross, we would have to drive west to the next checkpoint, which was three hours away. This rattled us slightly as it was now approaching midday on the last day on our visa, and we knew from experience how long these border crossings could take. My imagination went wild with the possible punishments for overstaying our visas.

Upon arriving at the new border crossing, we were met with bad news. A huge queue. The like you see on a bank holiday on the M25. The lorry drivers at the back had already been there for a number of days.

Weighing up the situation, we decided we'd rather take our chances with the lorry drivers than the border guards. So, we put up Audrey's windows and drove head down to the front of the queue, avoiding the mad gesticulations of everyone around us.

At the front, we explained our plight to the security guard and mercifully, he let us in. Which began another comically mad border crossing.

Now don't get me wrong, the British have done a pretty impressive job of messing up this part of the world. But fortunately for us, it was outside of living memory. There is a new bad man in town, and that is the Americans. And the hatred for them was impressive and, at times, wonderfully childish.

At the border post, they had taken the effort to construct a huge sign with every imaginable country printed onto it and next to each country was their cost of entry. To make a long story short, every country had the same cost of entry, except, you guessed it, for the Americans. Who's cost of entry was ten times higher.

What was impressive was not that they had decided to charge

the Americans more. They could have printed a sign that simply said Americans X, everyone else Y. The really impressive thing was they had taken the time to list out every other country, to really rub it into any passing American tourist.

And I, for one, am all for that level of childishness in international diplomacy. It should happen more often. I want to see it at the Port of Dover. "Sorry, Francoise — it's £100 for the French this week." Or maybe it would be better levied against the Australians dependent on recent Ashes results, or even the Germans for that matter, if they beat us in one more penalty shoot-out, "Sorry, Franz — it's £200 entry until the next World Cup. Well, you should have thought about that before you planted that penalty into the top corner." The money could be used to work out why we are so bad at penalties.

Fortunately for us Brits, the Premier League has erased all memory of our terrible deeds of the past. It's difficult to overestimate the brand of the Premier League overseas. As soon as anyone learns you're British, they start listing off premier league footballers at frightening speed. Frank Lampard usually plays for Arsenal and Wayne Rooney for Liverpool, but that doesn't matter; you're just so glad that Mohammed, with a wobbling AK-47 in his hand, has finally been convinced that you're not American.

In that sense, Wayne Rooney has probably done more to repair international relations and bring peace to Central Asia than George Bush. Thinking about it, most of us have done more for peace than George Bush just by doing absolutely nothing. But that would ruin the joke.

Maybe the Americans should start playing football, or good football in any case. That would probably do more for world peace than any of the last two presidencies combined.

So you can imagine our delight when the man in front of us at the border was an American who was being given a torrid time with form filling. No room for allied empathy here. We were swept through with relative ease and spat out on the other side of the border with thirty minutes to spare.

Both our heart rates returned to normal.

Enjoying the relief of Uzbekistan's canals

Withdrawing sufficient funds for a one night stay

Relaxing after a long drive, near the Afghanistan border

Beautiful Bukhara

16

Kazakhstan

Let me tell you, Kazakhstan is a dyslexics nightmare; I've misspelt it 49 times today alone. It's one of the many words, alongside "yacht" (which I only recently discovered the rest of you spell in that way), that cause me to fall down and worship the feet of whichever genius invented spellcheck, without which I would have been resigned to a career of hard manual labour.

The country has reached a level of fame unknown in the rest of central Asia, and that is all down to one man; Borat. And take my word for it, if you ever visit this nation, do NOT mention Borat. They hate him. They hate him with a vigour that I've never seen.

Borat, or more precisely Sacha Baron Cohen, labelled this country as the backwater of the world, a place of incest and antisemitism in equal measure. If you listen to Borat you would arrive on Kazakhstan's shores believing the national dish was horse meat and urine and that the nation's chief achievements are shooting dogs for sport, producing 300 tons of pubic hair a year, and exporting young boys to Michael Jackson's ranch.

The reason why such offence is taken – apart from the obvi-ous — is that Kazakhstan, compared to the rest of Central Asia, is actually a breakout economic success. Since declaring their independence from the Soviet Union in 1991, they've become the economic powerhouse of the region and this success is very much wrapped into their self-image. With newly found wealth comes an equal measure of self-consciousness. They look down their nose at the relatively underdeveloped neighbouring countries.

So, when Sacha Baron Cohen passed over Uzbekistan and Turkmenistan, or for that matter any of the other "Stans", and picked Kazakhstan as his nation of ridicule, it was close to a national disaster. They tried to have the film banned and even set up a government task force to try and counter the effects.

And to be fair to Kazakhstan, Borat's portrayal is more than a little unfair. They have made incredible strides in their short history. In 2003 47% of the population was living below the poverty line; today it's just 4%. So, after so much investment and progress, you can see why being labelled the world's laughingstock caused such irritation.

And indeed, big things are expected of Kazakhstan. The majority of its economic success has come from black gold, oil. Central Asia boasts the largest untapped energy reserves on the planet. And most of it is under Kazakh soil. If this supply is well managed, it is predicted to become one of the richest nations in the world. At which point, I'm sure, they plan on making Sacha Baron Cohen's life very hard for him.

However, as you've no doubt learnt by now, in Central Asia, that's only half the story. At the same time as making these economic strides, the president, Nazarbayev, has been making strides of his own. Most impressively, he has granted himself immunity from any law. Read that again. What he plans to do with his new found freedom is a question worth pondering. From speeding on the motorway to embezzling the proceeds of the nation's oil reserves, he is untouchable. Nazarbayev, it's also worth pointing out, had been in power for over twenty years when we arrived, even though the maximum term under their constitution is ten years. This fella obviously doesn't let irrelevant things like democracy get in the way of progress.

But if we rewind the clock, the history of this land is complex. Before the Soviets came, the area was not really a country at all, it was more a collection of tribes. But Stalin used a strategy known as the Great Terror to bully them into accepting Russian rule and loosely moulded the area into a nation-state. Dissenters were placed in concentration camps and systematically murdered. Generations of people were wiped out.

When the Soviet empire collapsed, the Russians left many things behind, including Anthrax and the Plague, which are kept in test tubes in a poorly guarded research facility under the watchful eye of a man who has, on national TV, openly offered to distribute his bounty amongst the population for the right price. It's worth pointing out this is all within a day's drive of the Taliban headquarters.

So it's fair to say this potent mix of untapped oil and terrorist armoury has piqued the interest of foreign governments in Borat's homeland.

One of the first things on our to-do list when arriving in a new country was to figure out what side of the road they drive on. This was easier said than done. We'd start by picking a side and driving with trepidation. Pulling away from the border, it was clear many of the other drivers were employing the same tactic. We'd all crawl away from the border post, waiting for someone with some local knowledge to take the lead and pick a side. Finally, someone with bigger balls than us would do so, and the rest of us, relieved to be in the chasing pack, would fall in line behind our leader, like a peloton in the Tour De France.

Usually, we'd hit the first corner only to be met by a border guard running late for his shift careering around the corner at breakneck speed, on our side of the road. As one, the peloton of cars would snake to the other side of the road, narrowly avoiding the tardy guard and correcting our course for the remainder of our time in that country.

We quickly realised that Kazakhstan was going to be a completely different kettle of fish to Uzbekistan. Its newfound wealth brought, as it does anywhere in the world, a certain level of crassness.

The traditional clothes we'd seen in Uzbekistan were replaced by Gucci and Prada advertisements pasted on people's chests. The humility and hospitality of Uzbekistan was replaced by fake tan, fake tits and easily bruised egos.

People who have just come into wealth seem to feel the need to emblazon it across themselves in the form of brands, skin tight clothing and fake tan, just to make sure everyone knows that they are indeed cashed up. The laughter and joyful happiness of Uzbekistan were replaced by solemn looks and menacing stares.

Kazakhstan seemed to be caught in an identity struggle, simultaneously trying to distance itself from the Arabs to the south and the Russians to the north, which left in their place a cultural vacuum.

Fortunately, we had the contact of a friend of Freddie's dad who happened to run the local airline (as you do). He had kindly welcomed us to come and stay at his place in Almaty, Kazakhstan's principal city. We headed there without delay.

As was our custom, upon reaching the outskirts of Almaty we flagged down a local taxi and asked him to drive us to the address we had been given. He was full of *yesses* and *of course sirs*, but it was clear he had no idea where we were going. After circumnavigating the city several times, he admitted defeat and pulled over to ask for help.

What followed was one of the charming oddities of these parts that repeated itself many times in various forms. The driver leaned out of his window and made a preliminary shout-out to whoever happened to be passing or sitting nearby to ask for directions. Before long, five or six men were at his car door, each speaking with substantial gesticulation, pointing and motioning around corners, roundabouts, up hills and down the other side. This was followed by much laughing, arm grasping and handshaking. The elder of the group then made a concerningly lengthy speech, making you think the address was just over the next mountain range.

Our taxi driver then got out of the car and thanked each of them individually and impassionedly, a further round of backslapping and handshakes followed and then emotional and protracted goodbyes were made as if they were family members preparing to leave for the front line.

Then they all went back to sitting down, ready for the next lost taxi driver. The whole ordeal must have taken 10 to 15 minutes.

Our driver came to our window.

"Did they know the place"? We asked.

"No."

We finally made it to the white-bricked enclave that would be our much-needed rest and relaxation for a few days.

And relax we did, falling into three days of slumber. We didn't see any of Almaty, and we were not sorry. We spent our days in air-conditioned luxury, lounging on the sofa by day and being entertained by our host by night. It was a real novelty to speak to someone at length who wasn't Freddie. Someone who actually got my jokes and laughed at them, or at least pretended to. And I'm sure Freddie felt the same way. I don't care how much you like someone; if you spent weeks on end confined in an ambulance in 40C heat, the Pope would get on your nerves.

At the beginning and end of each day, we would treat ourselves to a long and energy-restoring soak in the shower with water that spurted rather than dribbled.

Three days later, we were ready. Ready for our final assault.

Almaty sits close to the Chinese border, but to get there involved crossing the Himalayas. A match to no vehicle, let alone a retired ambulance from Manchester. Our plan, therefore, was to follow the road directly north to Russia and, more precisely, Siberia. From this frozen wasteland, we would have direct access to Mongolia and then to China through the Gobi Desert.

So north with headed. A few hours out of Almaty, Freddie made the dreadful discovery that one of the conditions of our visa was to register at a post office before leaving the country. This was one of the absurdities of this part of the world. Somehow, they had all convinced themselves that registering at a post office meant that you weren't a Western spy stealing state secrets or up to similar misdeeds.

Nonetheless, we would have to return to Almaty, complete the necessary bureaucracy and hit the road again with one less day to drive the 750 miles north to the border, which was now cutting it tight, to say the least.

The next day we rose early and hit the road hard. We had serious ground to cover in not a lot of time.

One of the most remarkable things about this trip was that for every mile we drove east of Istanbul, we never left a Chinese road. They had built the lot. It's called the Belt and Road Initiative, with China funding the construction of infrastructure projects in countries that can't afford them themselves. It's awesome in its ambition and, to many, terrifying. China is well on its way to owning and controlling the infrastructure in the majority of the eastern world.

That is not to say that the roads weren't a little shabby in places. These parts experience over sixty-degree temperature swings between summer and winter, which contorted the tarmac into all sorts of weird and wonderful shapes, all of which were less than ideal to drive on.

The lorry drivers drove these roads with a practised authority, though. They knew where the potholes were and dodged them effortlessly. Little consideration was given to traffic coming in the opposite direction, and it was up to you to get out of their way. If you're hit by a lorry that's driving on the wrong side of the road, well, that's your fault.

Our pace to the Russian Border was on track. But, and there's always a but isn't there, it was at that point that the Chinese government realised that tarmac was a waste of time, continually cracking under the temperature pressure. About halfway to the Russian border, it just stopped and was replaced by gravel, which dealt better with the temperature fluctuations, but brought its own complications and slowed our progress considerably.

The vibrations of the hard stone and sun-baked mud rattled us to our core, beating every last bit of marrow out of our bones and likely handing us expensive back and neck problems for life.

On the second day, we learnt the key was speed. At slow speed, you felt every rock and bump as your spine compressed and your head met your arse. But if you took these roads at speed, you would get good air, flying over the smaller bumps and crevices. Now, most of the damage was done to your teeth, constantly rattling like a gurning drug addict. But that was preferable in many ways. I prefer my spine to my teeth.

Often the road would end, and we would have to follow tyre tracks, which were frequently puzzling. Some would head off into the desert, while others would head the other way. None would carry on in the direction of the road. There's probably a reason for drivers taking the route they did, but we took our own path and headed in the direction we wanted to go. We quickly found out this was a bad idea as we hit a riverbed and deep sand, or was it mud? It was difficult to tell, and we cared little. A few hours later, we were reversing back out of our shallow grave after heavy shovelling — a mistake to learn from. Follow the local's tracks.

We followed the trodden path, and after a few more hours, feeling happy with our progress, Audrey's low wheel clearance came back to haunt us again.

The worn tracks on either side of the road got deeper and

deeper until the middle of the road rose up and grounded her by lifting up her underbelly and pulling the wheels clean off the road, leaving them spinning in mid-air. We glided for some heart-stopping distance like an oversized toboggan with no breaks. Mercilessly she stopped naturally and not into a wall or local pedestrian.

We got out and shovelled dirt into the tracks beneath her wheels and in front of her all the way along the rut to firmer ground to offer some traction. That seemed to do the trick — but for a moment there, we were utterly helpless.

It taught us never to follow the truck tracks caused by vehicles which had much higher ground clearance than us. The trick, we learned, was to always drive with one wheel up on the bank and the other on the raised ground between the two tracks. The resulting angle meant that you had more body weight pressed against the door when driving than on your seat, which caused nasty bruising to your arm and head. Razor concentration was necessary to stop slipping down into the tracks with an alarming jolt and a cracked skull.

Eventually, we left the ridges behind and re-joined our old friend, the teeth-shattering washboard road. But now we knew how to deal with her, "Foot to the floor and let her fly, Freddie!"

We compared our map with where we were. We estimated that we needed to cover another 100 miles today; how did we ever think we would cover that much road in these conditions? Well, I know exactly how. After about three seconds of consideration around a kitchen table with a cup of tea in hand, I can still hear Freddie say with a flick of the wrist, "It will be fine; how hard can driving be?". Well, let me tell you, damn hard. Harder than you can imagine. The heat tires you to your core; your sweaty hands can barely grip the steering wheel, your head pounds from dehydration and your bones ache from being pulverised by the rock-hard undulations of the road. This has as much in common with your air-conditioned morning commute as walking to the pub has in common with climbing Everest.

The struggle north was real. But we were captivated by it. We were consumed by our goal of reaching the Russian border.

The landscape was desolate; there was nothing. Like what I imagine the surface of the moon to look like. Ironically, many of the Soviet Union's moon landing attempts were made from these parts. Sometimes a camel or a man on a horse would appear with suspicion etched across his face. The fabled Islamic hospitality was waning — the people were getting more and more Russian by the day.

We had left the desert behind now completely; this was now what they call the Steppe. A fabled plain thousands of miles wide stretching from China in the east to the Caspian in the west. This was the land where Genghis Khan once ruled and carried out the most horrifying acts. It's estimated that he killed three-quarters of the population of this area, 10-15 million people.

The steppe was so flat that we could see impossible distances. You can take in whole weather systems. Out in front might be rain, but we could see where it started and where it finished. We could see the dark overhanging clouds and the shadows they cast over the landscape where the rain was about to hit, like a dark foreboding, and then when we traced our eyes along further, we could see the deluge, the straight dark lines of heavily falling rain and the poor landscape that was experiencing the infliction of the world's temper. And then, tracing further along the horizon, we met the bright sunshine that heralded in new hope; everything beneath it was a new shade of green and brightness.

Contrast is the joy of life. It makes things more than the sum of their parts. What is a hot summer's day without the drudgery of six months of rain and gales? What is tender chicken without its crispy skin? The refreshing first sip of ice-cold beer, without the long hot day of work.

We learnt many things about driving in these parts, most importantly, the police would pull us over whatever, so we might as well drive at speed to make up time.

Secondly, you don't drive with your pedals and steering wheel. You drive solely with the use of your horn. Or the Kazakh brake pedal, as we came to call it.

A bleat of the horn from a fellow road user could mean anything from "It's safe to overtake, please go ahead" to "If you overtake now, you'll be crushed by an oncoming truck."

The difference, we think, was in the length of the horn sound. But, if you're a novice in these parts, as we were, the only way to learn the intricacies of the language was to chance our arm.

When driving through villages, our chief concerns were camels, donkeys, goats and pedestrians crossing the road. We learnt, through trial and error, to stop for camels — they can make a big dent in your car and shouldn't be messed with — but to speed up for goats and pedestrians.

Pedestrians and goats will take advantage of even the slightest hesitation or touch of the brake. If we got stopped in the middle of a crowd of either, we would be surrounded within minutes and marooned for days; if you made this mistake with pedestrians, they also rinse you for every dime in your pocket.

We drove like hell through crowds of goats; they're slight on their feet and very difficult to hit.

We made good distance that day, but my God, did we work hard for it. By the time we admitted defeat for the day and made camp, we were battered and bruised on every possible body part; our skin slimed in sweat and dust.

Freddie took the opportunity to take some time for himself and headed out with the shovel and toilet paper.

Before progressing with this story, it's worth explaining the necessary shitting technique in this part of the world. Step 1, dig a hole (easier said than done on the barren Steppe). Step 2, do your business in the hole. Step 3, light the offending mess with a lighter. Step 4, bury anything left over.

Freddie had clearly got to step three when I heard the yelp.

I ran over to find him, pants around his ankles, madly trying to stamp out an infant bushfire spreading at frightening speed.

I didn't ask him whether he'd yet had the chance to wipe.

I joined him in jumping up and down on the flames as they spread from scrub to bush. It was hopeless; the fire was spreading far quicker than we could contain it.

With some quick thinking, we dug a trench at one end, pulling up any flammable dried-out scrubs that were acting as kindling.

That seemed to do the job, on one side. We raced across and did the same to the other. The fire continued to rage, but at least it was contained. And within thirty minutes it started to burn out and Freddie could go back to his business and finally pull up his pants.

The poor man will never take a shit again.

I have to admit, Russia wasn't a country we were looking forward to. Particularly as the only part we would see was Siberia, which brought up visions of freezing winters, Gulags and Siberian Tigers. The plan was to cross the border at a town named Semey and then traverse Siberia west to east, passing Lake Baikal, until we met the border with Mongolia.

We left the flatness of the Steppe behind as the road to the border winded through the Altai Mountains, which were spectacular, snow-capped and heralded in a drop in temperature.

We heard a patter on the windshield. At first, I couldn't put my finger on what it was; it felt like a distant memory resurfacing. The face of an old friend whose name I couldn't quite remember. The rate of the patter increased, and then it hit me. "Rain!" I shouted and grabbed Freddie's arm. I pulled over, jumped out of the van, and looked up to the sky, arms out and swirled around like a lunatic letting the soft refreshing droplets soak me. It was the first rain we'd had since that damn mountaintop in Georgia, and it was as refreshing as drinking a cold beer on a summer's day.

But the dream quickly turned into a nightmare. The rain churned up the hard mud road into a quagmire. Audrey's tires couldn't grip and spun through the sludge as she groaned her displeasure. By the afternoon, the road was a running stream. Progress was slow, and Audrey's white paint job became splattered with thick brown mud.

We reached the border just after lunch with plenty of nerves. The thought of Russian border guards filled me with dread.

As if to confirm our worries, the border guards sported bruises and scars that, if you were unfamiliar with these parts, you'd assumed were war memories but were more likely the only remaining memory of Friday night.

One such bruised border guard looked at our passports and then at us, not with any intensity; he just looked through us with the blurred eyes of boredom. He licked the top of his ballpoint pen and started copying out our passport details in a vast leather-bound book. The same way he had done 100s of times a day for a countless number of days. He'd certainly lost count.

Finally, he got out his battered stamp and beat the page in frustration. The first emotion we'd seen from this man. He looked back up to us and rubbed his forefinger and thumb together, $40 to cross. Daylight robbery, a month's wages around these parts, but, seeing the state of the place, I didn't blame them. Squeeze these Western tourists for every dollar they can afford. Although how much of it would make it past our new friend, was another question entirely.

Transaction over, he motioned for us to move onto the next counter for yet more illegible scrawl and stamping. After forty-five minutes of this, we were free to go. And just like that, we were into Russia, our twenty-first country of the trip and, all being well, our third last.

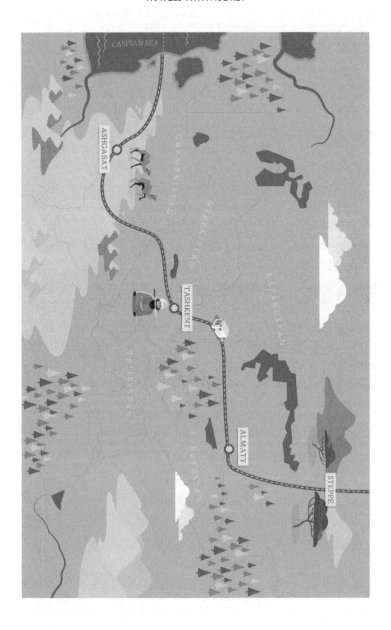

17

Siberia

We crossed the border high-fiving each other; it felt like a huge moment in our trip, the end of Central Asia. The end of constant sand in our eyes, the end of the ridiculous heat, the end of two-item menus. The desert had tried its hardest and thrown everything at us, from wandering terrorists to suicidal camels, but we had emerged the other side battered, certainly, but very much intact. It felt like the hardest bit was over, and it was downhill from there on in. We were ready for anything that the Russians, Mongols, or Chinese could throw at us.

Crossing into Siberia, we left behind the harsh conditions and climbed into dense forest, trees tapping on the windows as we drove, dousing the light. The relief of cooler climbs was quickly replaced by actual coldness, and we scrambled for our jumpers and jackets for the first time in two months.

Siberia really was miserable, I'm sorry to be so negative, but Christ alive, you wouldn't want to live here. If you're over the age of sixteen, it seems it's mandatory to have a bottle of vodka stapled to your hand at all times, if you're under the age of 16, it's just highly encouraged.

Smiles were not common; even in the bridal party we drove past getting married on exit sixteen of the major freeway. The bride's white dress spattered by the mud flung from passing cars. It was grey, it was freezing cold, spitting with rain, and it was the height of summer.

"You're lucky you didn't come in the winter," the border guard mumbled.

During the trip, we developed an unofficial quality-of-life index based on the roadside produce. In Georgia, they sold an amazing variety of fruit and vegetables, bursting with colour and sold with smiles. In central Asia, it was Dates, millions of them stacked up on the side of the road. We gorged ourselves, and I haven't been able to eat one since.

In Siberia, however, the roadside produce were cigarettes. Sold individually. Is there ever a more depressing sight? And cans, not bottles, of vodka. The use of a can suggests to me that they were designed to be drunk neat and in one sitting, perhaps even in one gulp.

The locals don't like anyone that's not Russian and preferably not from outside of Siberia. They're hard-drinking, tough men who have had difficult lives and like to tell you about it. There's something of a camaraderie that comes from living through hard times. I've noticed it in other parts of the world. You can look into your neighbours' eyes and know they've had it just as hard as you have, and they've lasted too. And to that very tone, anyone who isn't from "here" hasn't had to tough it like us and isn't to be trusted.

You probably don't need me to tell you that the Siberians don't take much pride in their roads. We averaged 5mph in many stretches. Potholes like you've never seen. Dodging cars, vans and even tractors that had met their match and then just left to rust in the middle of the road.

At the end of the day, we got out to review Audrey's condition. Ever since the forgotten key incident where we had to break into Audrey by ripping off her sunroof (I'll take the blame for that one), we had used an Ascot Racecourse umbrella to act as cover, popping it through the exposed hole and opening it up, which must have been a bizarre sight. However, unsurprisingly, this was no match for the Siberian rain. It had got in, and it had got in everywhere. Everything was soaked through, from our clothes to our beds to our sleeping bags. The rain had combined with the residual dust from the desert to make mud so thick it wouldn't budge. It was going to be a long, miserable night.

We wrapped ourselves in our cold, wet blankets and tried to sleep through the shivers. The rain didn't relent, streaming through our makeshift roof. Waking with a start every time an especially big drop landed on my face.

Ever since we had to rip off that sunroof, I'd struggled to sleep, envisioning people dropping in from above and landing knees apart, pinning down my arms whilst they slowly removed the dagger from between their teeth. On several occasions, I could swear I could see a face looking down from the darkness above. Any nighttime bang or rustle was my murderer-to-be beginning his ascent of the bonnet. I laid on my back, wide awake, with dinner-plate-sized eyes, for hours on end whilst Freddie contently snored.

We woke up in the morning miserable and to a primaeval swamp. Thick mud came halfway up Audrey's wheels. A quick pump on the accelerator confirmed our fears — there was to be no shifting her — we would have to dig our way out.

Using our shit shovel, we started to scrape away at the mud. The thickness of it required all our strength and weight to separate it from the tires and to make a track back to the road. After an hour of digging, we tried again, the wheels still span, back to digging.

After another hour, we gave up; we couldn't dig through to any sort of firm ground to allow Audrey to get traction on her tires. Exhausted and covered in mud, we laid in the back. Our positivity at crossing central Asia had been completely extinguished. Russia presented a completely different challenge. But I'll be damned if this trip ends in a Siberian trench.

Next to try were the carpets that we hadn't used since that damned hill in Istanbul.

I put them under Audrey's back wheels. And shouted, "Hit the gas, Freddie!" More wheel spin, and the carpets flicked nonchalantly out of the way. Damn.

"Let's try again."

This time I really forced them under the wheels as best I could.

"Gas Freddie!"

Wheel spin...but then suddenly the carpet took hold and was forced under the wheels like a factory conveyor belt, and Audrey shunted backwards about a metre until the carpet ran out and the wheels spun once more. Buoyed by our meter gain, I ran back around and placed the carpets back under her wheels.

"Okay, and again Freddie!"

One meter more.

The carpets, getting heavier and heavier with the build-up of mud, now needed Freddie's strength as well to lift them to the back.

One metre more. We repeated this again and again until finally, about an hour later, we made it back to the road. Relieved and covered in mud, we got back in the van and continued to head east.

A day of monotony commenced. The road dissected through miles upon miles of thick Siberian forest. The odd car going in the other direction was the only break from the tedium. Driven by a burning desire to just get out of this fucking country, we carried on east, never taking a break. *Let's just get this done*, I thought.

There is something terrifying about forests. A primaeval fear that has been buried deep into our subconsciousness. You know the fear is deeply stupid and lacking in logic. But still, you can't shake it. Every time I get out of Audrey to take a pee, set up a stove or check her tyres, I felt like I am being watched by thousands of unseen eyes from just beyond the darkness of the receding forest. Every crack was the footstep of some vengeful Siberian forgotten by the modern world.

The trees were so large and close together it was suffocating, claustrophobic even. If you were up in an aeroplane, the view would have been awesome, trees teeming with life coating the undulating hills for as far as you can see. But down here, it's repressive and dark and makes my imagination run wild.

It is difficult to explain just how bad the roads in Siberia actually are. In places, the only difference between the "road" and the field was that the road had more potholes. And these potholes had become more like craters. We could only average about 10 mph as the rain turned the mud-covered roads into slush.

At the end of that tortuously slow day, bones and teeth dislodged from their rightful places, we stopped and hobbled around the back wanting to just slide into bed without dinner, thinking, hoping, that tomorrow would be a better day. Which was when we first smelt it. The smell of diesel.

And not just the normal diesel smell from cars; it hit us like a knockout punch as we walked around the back. We checked the tank under Audrey, no sign of any issues or cracks. We opened Audrey's back door, and bang, we were hit by it, fumes of diesel so strong we had to turn away and shield our faces. Intoxicating fumes that made us wretch.

And then I saw it, one of our spare tanks had ruptured and spilt its messy contents everywhere, on our pots and pans, through our clothes, our sleeping bags, it had seeped into the carpet, everywhere.

It was a bloody miracle that the vibrations of the road hadn't struck two things against each other, caused a spark, and blown us all back to Oxford.

We couldn't get in the back without suffocating. We'd try and then retreat. Taking deep breaths, we grabbed what we could, discarded the most soaked items, and then shut her up for good. No more sleeping inside for us.

So that night, we built up a massive fire, as big as we could get it, and set it alight, sending sparks and flames high into the night sky. Praying that it would burn through the night and give us warmth. It didn't; we woke up at 2 am to the final embers and shivered through the rest of the night.

Our mood was at an all-time low. We barely spoke to each other, grunting instructions when necessary and getting irritated by the smallest of infringements. Ever since we had crossed into Russia, it just seemed like one thing after another. We longed for the heat of the desert once more.

But just as that depth hit, we rolled over a hilly top and gazed upon Lake Baikal. Lake Baikal had become almost mythical to us over the last few days. It is one of the largest lakes in the world, holding over a third of the world's fresh water. And it's an awesome sight to see stretched out in front of you in all her glory. But to us, she was more than that. She signalled our final day in Siberia. The Mongolian border was within touching distance. We got out to take her in. She caught us just in time, like the world knew we needed a pick-me-up.

Rejuvenated by her splendour, we pulled over to feast upon some locally caught fish. Delicious fresh tender white meat cooked over coals. It was the first fish we'd eaten since leaving Europe, and we gobbled it up and felt the warmth of good food for the first time in days.

After lunch, we dived into the lake, shrieking like little girls as we submerged ourselves in her icy waters and washed the mud off our bodies. We were told by locals that the lake was so cold that bacteria couldn't live in the water, making it safe to drink so we filled up all our spare water containers from the lake and drank even more.

I knew I was in trouble before the hour was up. Seeing the shock in my eyes as I grabbed his shoulder Freddie pulled over, and I leapt out of the cab just in time to pull my pants down in full view of the road. I don't want to ruin your lunch, so I won't go any further with my descriptions. But just know that it was bad. Very bad. The water, it turns out, was not safe to drink. Not for our soft western bellies, in any case.

Completely incapacitated, I sat in the passenger seat, only moving to motion to Freddie to stop Audrey to get out to do similar misdeeds. Progress to the Mongolian border was slow as I left my mark on the Siberian landscape. My newfound enthusiasm was lost as I squirmed restlessly, holding my aching belly.

As we neared the Mongolian border, we reached the final

rise of the Altai mountains and pulled over to view all that lay before us. After talking about her for months, aching for her in Siberian forests, there she was. Mongolia. Like the Garden of Eden stretched out in front of us. Rolling, grass-topped hills as far as the eye could see, interrupted only by herds of wild horses who had made this radiantly green land their home. As if only to make this moment more symbolic, the dark, forbidding clouds that hung over Siberia behind us had cleared, and the sunlight streamed from above to create every shade of green imaginable.

We wound our way down the final hill in Siberia and made camp a few miles out from the border. An amazing spot on the banks of a lake. That night the fire lasted until morning, and we awoke with smiles on our faces for the first time in a week.

Getting ready for another cold night

And another, this time with the Ascot umbrella in view

18

Mongolia

I've got something to admit to you. We have a dark secret that we've been keeping from you and, most shockingly, from Audrey all this time. She isn't going to make it to China. Our dream isn't going to be a reality.

Back in Georgia, at the Chinese Embassy, we were informed it would cost us $10,000 to get Audrey into China. $10,000 that we didn't have. And like a dog owner given a choice between an unaffordable vet bill or euthanasia, we faced an impossible choice.

She had transported us gallantly across every conceivable landscape. She sped us along the motorways of Europe, creaked her way up the mountains of Georgia, sweated her way through the heat of the desert and at every turn protected us from the dangers that surrounded. Like a horse winning the Grand National with an amateur jockey, her nimble footwork and determination got us here. And she got us here in spite of us. In spite of our best efforts to ruin the journey at every turn. But now we were faced with abandoning her within sight of the finish line.

As much as we tried to put it to the back of our minds, in reality, we had already made the decision. We knew there was no way we were going to spend that amount of money. We just hadn't admitted it to ourselves yet. And we hadn't told Audrey yet.

And so Mongolia, it was decided, would be her new home. We had arranged, through a charity back home, that the Ulaanbaatar Children's hospital would take her on to ferry stricken kids to and from hospital. It was a heart-warming arrangement, knowing that she would be back doing what she does best, helping people. But it didn't make the prospect of saying goodbye any easier.

Leaving a British ambulance in a developing country comes with its fair share of bureaucracy. It was a process that could melt the most optimistic of souls. Form after form after form after form was handed out, filled in and then promptly rejected for missing a box here or there. Back of the queue you go. It came to me to run this process, of course, it did, whilst Freddie kept himself busy topping up his tan.

The whole border crossing took ten hours. TEN HOURS!

Upon completing the final form and receiving that sweet, final, stamp of approval from our last border guard, I burst through the doors into the Mongolian sunshine to find Freddie conducting an auction from the back of Audrey.

He was standing out of the back door with a milieu of people looking up at him as he took bids from the crowd like an auctioneer at Sotheby's. Bang, he slapped Audrey's back door to signify the winning bid and pointed to the proud new owner.

The tow rope, our vital jump leads, the spare fuel containers (along with their holes) and my Liverpool scarf (!) had all been auctioned off to the highest bidder, the majority of which had been snapped up by the Mongolian border guards. I let Freddie know that I thought this was tempting fate a little, especially as Audrey's battery was beginning to fail, and we still had a couple of hundred miles left, but it was too late. The deals had been struck, and the new owners had long since disappeared.

Nevertheless, we burst onto the Mongolian Steppe with tears in our eyes; our final border had been crossed with Audrey, which brought a feeling of both relief and sadness. We were so close now to achieving our goal, a goal that no one thought realistic.

But with the dedication and focus it took to make it this far, we never actually stopped to think about what reaching Mongolia meant. It meant the end of freedom, the end of constant travelling, the end of experiencing new cultures every day, meeting people, and seeing sights that few would ever get the chance to.

The most wonderful thing of all about long-term travel was the serenity of lack of commitments. There were no events to attend or organise. No one to impress nor disappoint. All that was required of us was the slow trudge east. To be a little closer to our goal at the end of the day than at the start.

When the sun rises, you wake up; when it starts its descent, you turn off the road. Everything in between was just one hand on the steering wheel, the other out the window and your foot on the accelerator.

You're neither alert nor distant; you're tranquil, something unachievable in the stresses of everyday life. Yes, there had been tough days, of course, but the reward and satisfaction we got from overcoming those obstacles would be hard to replace.

We also hadn't stopped to think about the new chapter this achievement would herald in. In a week, we would be in an air-conditioned office in central London, answering to soul-dead career men. A new life of the 9-to-5, of annual holiday limits and monthly performance reviews.

In retrospect, Freddie was the perfect person for the trip. His enthusiasm for life and for new, especially risky, experiences is unbounded. We were thrust together through a lack of alternative options for other travelling companions. But no matter, I wouldn't have had it any other way. The most important ingredient to any situation is enthusiasm and a positive mindset; we wouldn't have gotten there without it.

We turned off the road and headed out onto the steppe. The ground was firm and manicured by the roaming horses; it wouldn't have looked out of place on the 18th green at St Andrew's. And it provided plenty of support for our childish zeal for some off-roading.

Audrey had never sounded better, roaring across the deserted landscape in search of, we weren't quite sure what. We went racing up peaks and down the other side. We sped along riverbanks as we screamed out of the windows like madmen. Fred, not one to waste a photo op, posed with his QPR scarf extending above his head, standing atop Audrey, in the belief that this was the furthest a QPR scarf had been from Loftus Road. I reminded him that QPR scarfs rarely leave west London, but he didn't find that funny.

From the top of one such peak, we spotted a valley in the distance with a river and wooded area, the perfect spot for our final few nights with Audrey. Descending that hill towards our last campsite was possibly the happiest we had been all trip. After all, we had been through, a booze-addled run through Europe, nearly being boiled in Turkmenistan, kidnapped at knifepoint in Uzbekistan, before risking life and limb on those

Siberian roads, we were finally in striking distance of our goal. For the first time we could actually relax and have some level of confidence we were going to make it.

We parked up alongside the lake and wasted no time diving straight in. The water, which had followed us down off the Siberian mountains, was freezing, but only served to enliven us further. We had dreamed about this in that pub back in Oxford all those months ago. Lying on our backs, gazing at the blue sky and surrounding peaks, not a sound but the wind, as we gently flowed downstream. This was freedom.

With enough supplies to last a few days, plenty of wood for the fire, water from the lake, and only having given our welcoming party in Ulaanbaatar very loose arrival dates, we had no plans to leave for a few days at least.

Cooking up breakfast the next morning, we noticed a group of Mongols approaching our camp from a distance. We had long ago lost any amazement on the ability of the locals in this part of the world to randomly show up on foot when the nearest settlement was many miles away. After a quick tour of Audrey and her now almost full sleeve of tattoos, we invited them to join us for breakfast, which they heartily accepted, but they had no plans on eating.

After an hour or so of gestures and loose attempts to speak in broken English on their part and with us in return speaking in equally broken English but onsetting an attempt at a heavy Mongolian accent (is this embarrassing tactic of putting on your counterpart's accent in an attempt to be understood an exclusive trait of the English?) it was decided by the Mongolians that this was a waste of everyone's time and a drinking bout would be far more productive. Or, probably far more likely, this was their intention from the outset.

One of the members revealed a bottle of vodka from his person, and we set about it.

It became apparent that the Mongolians took their drinking very seriously and we dared not interrupt their strict process. First, the vodka was poured, with, as the bout progressed, increasingly little concern as to how much vodka would end up in your glass. Then all drinks were raised, some distant God was praised and honoured, mugs smashed together aggressively, heads tossed back, and vodka tipped down throats. Followed up with as manly a scream as you could muster.

When it came to Freddie's turn, not being the most God-fearing of men, he panicked and praised QPR's current striker Abel Tarrabat, which caused me to spit my vodka all over my neighbour in shock, which only seemed to increase the pace of the proceedings, realising that we were as depraved and sick as they were. Everyone raised their glasses, shouted "ADEL TARRABAT!" and threw their heads back.

We tossed off our rigidity with abandon and suddenly were able to communicate in a way not possible before. New friendships were formed, and everyone was back-slapping each other as if we had known each other for years.

Now and then, one of them would fall asleep in the grass beside us, only to return an hour later with new thirst and vigour.

Any reasonable person would baulk at several shots of vodka before you've had your cornflakes, but it's amazing how quickly you become accustomed to it.

We delayed our planned arrival into Ulaanbaatar for a further twenty-four hours, reasoning that it wouldn't be wise to arrive at a Children's hospital in this state.

We awoke the following morning with heavy heads and with our Mongol counterparts laid about in the grass around the van, glasses still in hand, snoring loudly.

We cleared up camp with the intention of starting the emotional final leg of our trip to Ulaanbaatar. But the noise woke our neighbours, and they were having none of it.

We were to spend the next few days with their family in their Yurt in the neighbouring valley. Driven either out of genuine hospitality or a clever ruse to get a free lift home, we weren't sure, but we accepted heartily in any case.

They climbed aboard and directed us across the hills to the spectacular valley they had chosen to be their home for the summer.

We spotted it a while before we arrived. Tiny spots of perfectly white yurts against the green backdrop of the surrounding steppe, hills rising behind.

We arrived as mum, dad, grandma, along with various other family members streamed out to meet us. How they knew that we were coming or who we were without phones, we never knew, but they couldn't have been more welcoming.

The camp included several ponies, only slightly taller than your hip but built like a brick wall and capable of carrying even the roundest of Mongols, and Mongols can be very round. Goats were also part of the family, and, most amazing of all, a flock of reindeer and a golden eagle, used for hunting mountain foxes way above us on nearby climbs, made up the final members of this motley crew.

The smile and warmth of their greeting is something that will stay with us for some time.

After formal introductions, tea was served inside the main yurt. Stepping under the doorway and into these yurts was like entering a different world. The sides were decorated in a million and one colours with rugs adorning the walls and huge trunks, so large it made you wonder how they transported them with the changing of seasons, ornately painted in blues, reds and yellows. And at the top, a window to the sky that would be opened to let the sun shine through and further highlight the artwork.

At the centre of the yurt was always a wood-burning stove with a chimney leading out, which had a mixed success rate. Sometimes the simple act of brewing up some tea would force you stumbling for the door to get out before you inhaled a lung full of smoke.

Once tea was over, clearly unsure what to do with two Westerners for the afternoon, they handed us two of their ponies and pointed out in the direction of a hill to explore.

I'm sure, assuming that everyone above the age of five could ride as well as they could, they thought this would be a great way for us to explore their country.

Luckily for them, they were half right; one of us could ride. The other, Freddie, had gone sheet white, clearly recalling some unfortunate previous experiences.

The fact that Freddie's mount was in a very irritable mood that morning only improved the situation in my head. This was going to be a fun day.

It started well enough until we crossed into the next valley and stumbled upon our host's neighbouring clan, who wasn't so hospitable. Our welcoming party consisted of a pair of attack dogs that our mounts did not take kindly to and bolted across the landscape in retreat, ignoring our desperate tugs on the reins.

Now, fortunately for Freddie, the Mongolian saddle was

nothing like its Western cousin. Viewed side on it's shaped like a "V", and you wedge your body in between the two wings. So designed, certainly not for comfort, but so that the Mongolian archers could ride and fire their arrows facing backwards just as well as they could facing forwards.

This design, with Freddie's body wedged into the saddle, saved him, initially. But there's little a rider can do when the girth, the piece of rope securing the saddle around the horse's midriff, snaps.

The saddle went one way, Freddie the other.

Freddie hit the ground with a thump and a whimper. I had an immediate decision to make, chase after the horse and leave Freddie for the dogs, or stop and see if he's okay and lose the horse. I chose the former — not wanting to offend our hosts by returning with one less steed.

From his worried expression as I looked back over my shoulder and the shout of "MAX!!" — I could tell he didn't completely agree with my decision.

Fortunately, when I returned with his mount, he was bruised and battered, but not mauled.

Fred didn't share my rosy outlook and sent some expletives in my direction as he dropped the stick he had been using to defend himself, fixed the girth, and jumped back onboard.

After the initial excitement, we took a more sedentary pace as we roamed around the Steppe. The landscape of rolling green hills, hundreds of wild horses and running rivers was so spectacular that it even lifted Freddie's foul mood.

It felt like there wasn't another person for thousands of miles.

When we returned to the camp, we were greeted by quite the

affair. The sons of the family had returned, having rounded up their reindeer. Having never set eye on one before today, I can tell you they were quite spectacular animals. Smaller than you expect, with furry antlers and incredibly inquisitive, nuzzling their noses in your pockets searching for food. These poor guys will give the family food and warmth over the freezing winter months.

That night we were the guests of honour and, as is custom, were invited to slaughter the goat for our evening meal.

I'm no vegetarian but killing a goat was not on my bucket list. I told myself to pull myself together. If I was willing to eat it, I should be willing to kill it.

Whilst Freddie held its haunches I (whilst apologising profusely to the poor animal) picked up the serrated knife given to me, counted to ten, and slit its throat. A river of blood shot out from between my fingers, splattering onto my feet, still warm from its body. I felt the animal's legs buckle and strain against my grip. I let the poor thing slide to the floor in a heap. It was over.

Let me tell you; I love the Mongolians. They were endlessly hospitable and are only challenged by the Japanese for humility and grace. But they cannot cook. I have never been to such a place with consistently foul food. I would not wish it on my worst enemy. If we weren't there of our own free will, and had quite often chosen the dish from a menu and paid for it, it would be considered torture. And I'm sorry to say; this came to full bear in that yurt.

The ordeal of killing the goat was child's play compared to eating it.

Looking forward to a beautifully barbecued leg of goat, we were horrified to be presented with boiled stomach filled with the poor goat's lung, heart and intestines.

Judging by the proud smiles as the plates were put down in front of us, this was quite the delicacy. And guessing by the pungent meaty smell, the way to cook these things was as briefly as possible and using few other ingredients to mask the flavour of the star of the show, innards.

I hadn't eaten all day, but my appetite had left me. It had crawled back into Audrey and returned to England. This meal was going to have to be forced down.

The family watched Freddie and I in nervous anticipation as I raised the first spoonful to my mouth. The unmistakable smell of insides filled my nostrils as it reached my lips.

"Do. Not. Gag" I told myself.

I opened my mouth, put the spoon inside and gently slid it back out. My cheeks bulged full of intestines, stomach lining and blood. I closed my eyes and breathed slowly through my nose to regain composure.

"Okay, swallow in 3", I said to myself. "1, 2...3!"

I took a big breath in through my nose and swallowed. No, it wasn't a swallow it was more of a chug. A huge forceful chug with prayers and pleading attached. I felt the intestine slipping down my throat. So far, so good. But then, a piece of congealed blood brushed my tonsils. I tried to breathe again to calm my emotions, but as I did, my nostrils were overwhelmed by the smell of blood. The pungent, meaty smell of fresh warm blood. I opened my eyes in panic. I could feel it coming. There was nothing I could do. My body was about to be taken over by the unconscious, by instinct. I jumped up and rushed to the door holding my mouth like a teenager after his first shot of tequila. I burst through it and retched onto their porch. Throwing my hands forward to try and propel the ungodly liquid as far from their front door as possible. First, a little bit and then as the half-digested food filled my nostrils once more, I retched again, emptying the contents of my stomach all over the entrance to their home.

Bent over, I took a moment to compose myself. Slowly, my breathing returned to normal. I wiped my mouth with the back of my sleeve.

I turned around to a room filled with silence, everyone's eyes on me. Our chef's mouth wide open in horror. Freddie squirmed in the awkwardness. And then their daughter started to cry.

The following morning, we bid our goodbyes in a cloud of embarrassment.

"For fucks sake, Max," Freddie said through gritted teeth as the door slammed and he waved to our hosts.

* * *

And so began the final day of our trip. After a few days off, Audrey needed a little assistance to get warmed up but then spluttered into life and happily motored down her final road, content in her ignorance of what lay in store. Freddie and I sat in silence.

My thoughts drifted to the naysayers; the "not a chancers," the "the only way you're going to make it to China is in a fucking box"-ers. I had long dreamed of parading triumphantly on our return, like holding the FA Cup aloft in front of rival fans. But I had moved past that. I have come to realise that the vast majority of people give advice not to guide you but to confirm their own actions (or lack thereof, most likely). There are few greater freedoms in life than letting go of the need to convince others of your own decisions. Let them disagree and ridicule; that's when you know you're on an interesting path.

A sign welcoming us to Ulaanbaatar faded into sight through tear-fogged eyes. We drove silently through the industrial suburbs and then further into the traffic-stained centre. Not a word was said.

Our first stop was to the mechanics to ensure our erratic driving hadn't caused irreparable damage to Audrey. The last thing we would want was for her to break down whilst ferrying someone to the hospital. But aside from a few superficial defects, she passed with flying colours. We beamed with pride. An ambulance designed to brave the icy winters of Manchester had traversed some of the most inhospitable deserts in the world driven by two of the most incompetent mechanics you could find and lived to tell the tale.

It was then a short drive across town to the drop-off location. Freddie and I would catch a train the following morning to Beijing to complete our trip. But this felt like the end. Saying goodbye to Audrey would mark the end of our adventure in our minds. It didn't feel right to carry on without her. From there on, we were just on our way home.

It felt like we were driving a much-loved dog to the vet for the final time. We arrived and shook a few hands, and had our photos taken. We smiled and talked politely, but we weren't really there. I had thought about this moment countless times over the last three months. In my mind, we would be standing on a podium spraying champagne over each other and a baying crowd. But in the podium's place was just sadness. I wanted to get back in, turn the ignition, and drive Audrey to our next country and our next adventure.

But instead, we packed a rucksack each, gave her one last tap on the bonnet, signed our names on her side, like countless more had done before us, turned our backs and walked off in search of the train station.

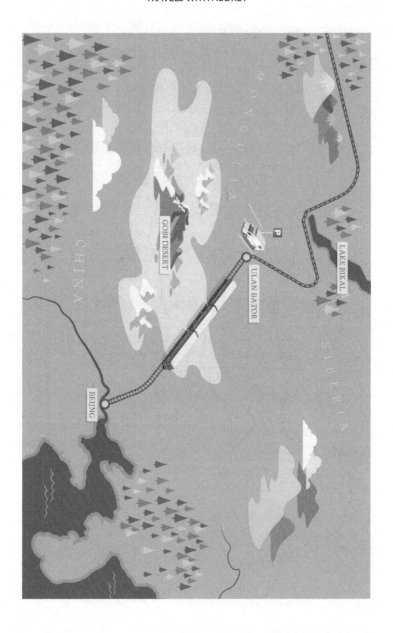

The extraordinary beauty of Mongolia

Audrey off roading!

Our final camping spot before arriving in Ulaanbaatar

Freddie trying to tame the resident reindeers

Our final day, before Freddie's fall

Our final supper before my embarrassment

19

Epilogue

Max and Freddie are still good friends, best men at each other's wedding and have had many adventures since. Max didn't last long in the world of the 9-to-5, never getting on board with annual leave and performance reviews and now charts his own course in the world of entrepreneurship. Freddie is still clinging on resolutely, rising through the ranks. And as for Audrey, last heard, she is still ferrying sick kids to hospital, the star of their fleet and trusted in all conditions. Although unfortunately, she did have to shed her tattoos before her first day.

Printed in Great Britain
by Amazon

17160362R00159